Then Comes Marriage

Then Comes Marriage

A NOVELLA

Angela Hunt and Bill Myers

ZondervanPublishingHouse
Grand Rapids, Michigan

A Division of HarperCollins*Publishers*

Then Comes Marriage
Copyright © 2001 by Angela Elwell Hunt and Bill Myers

Requests for information should be addressed to:

ZondervanPublishingHouse
Grand Rapids, Michigan 49530

Library of Congress Cataloging-in-Publication Data

Hunt, Angela Elwell, 1957–
    Then comes marriage / Angela Hunt and Bill Myers.
      p. cm.
    ISBN: 0-310-23016-0
    1. Married people—Fiction. 2. Young adults—Fiction.
I. Myers, Bill, 1953– . II. Title.
PS3558.U46747 T48 2001
813'.54-dc 21

                00-049992
                CIP

This edition printed on acid-free paper.

Published in association with the literary agency of Alive Communications,
Inc., 7680 Goddard Street, Suite 200, Colorado Springs, CO 80920.

Interior design by Rob Monacelli

Printed in the United States of America

---

00 01 02 03 04 /❖ DC/ 10 9 8 7 6 5 4 3 2 1

For Gary,

Who for twenty years has made every day
an adventure

—Angie

For Brenda,

A more faithful friend could never be
found

—Bill

Chapter One

"What do you mean, you've made a horrible mistake?"

Heather thought her mother's voice seemed to come from far away, or maybe the problem was the clogged feeling in her ears. She couldn't hear anyone when she was crying.

All the words she had rehearsed in the car jumbled together and came out in a broken wail as she lifted her tear-blurred gaze to meet her mother's. "It's Kurt! I never should have married him! I thought I could tough it out, but this time he's gone too far!"

Her mother reached out from the doorway, quick to draw her into the privacy of the house, but Heather didn't care if she woke all of Pinehurst Drive with her wailing. All the neighbors had been at her wedding last year when Mr. and Mrs. Kurt Stone were born; it seemed only right that they should witness Mr. and Mrs. Kurt Stone's dismal death.

"Shh, honey, come on in," Mrs. Irvin said, her arm falling around her daughter's shoulders with affectionate familiarity.

Heather sobbed anew, realizing that Kurt's embrace had felt that tender—once. She'd probably never feel his arm around her again.

Mrs. Irvin shut the front door with a forceful shove, then pulled Heather into the living room. Wiping her streaming eyes, Heather saw her father standing in the kitchen doorway, his tattered robe loosely tied around his paunch. The long strands of his silver hair wavered in the kitchen's fluorescent light.

"Can't a body sleep in on a Saturday morning?" His voice emerged as a gravelly croak, but his eyes glimmered with anxious alarm. "What's come over you, girl?"

"Hush, dear, go back to bed. I'm making our daughter a cup of tea." Mom moved toward the kitchen, nudging Heather's bewildered father out of the way as she moved through the doorway.

For her dad's sake, Heather tried to rein in her emotions. "I'm okay, Daddy." She gave him a quivering smile. "As long as you haven't rented out my bedroom, that is. I may need it for a few days. Just until I can get a place of my own—"

"Frankie!" he yelled over his shoulder, cutting her off. "You'd better fix this! Here I am trying to get rid of Billy, and Heather wants to move back in!"

Heather pressed her fingers to the bridge of her nose and closed her eyes, trying to resist the fresh wave of sorrow that wanted to pour out her eyes, her mouth, her heart. What was it with men? Here she was, trying to crawl back into the bosom of her family for comfort, and her father acted as though he wanted to put up a barbed-wire fence to keep her out.

"Come into the kitchen, honey," Mom called, her voice amazingly cheerful for someone whose only daughter had just confessed that her marriage was a sham and her entire life a disaster. "Let's have tea at the kitchen table so your father can go back to bed."

Gulping back hot tears, Heather moved past her father and automatically slid into the kitchen chair she had vacated right after high school graduation. She sat silently, fingering the tattered edge of a faded plastic place mat, until the teakettle whistled. Her mother moved to quiet it, then looked at her daughter. In her glance Heather saw compassion mingled with something that looked suspiciously like humor.

She wouldn't think this was funny for long.

"Tell me all about it, Heather," she said, switching off the stove as she lifted the kettle. "I've got all morning, so you can just take your time and tell me everything. I'm assuming you and Kurt had a fight?"

Too shattered to speak, Heather nodded.

"A fight is not the end of the world." Mom poured the steaming water into two mugs and lifted a brow. "So, what did you fight about? Money?"

Heather shook her head as her eyes filled again. How could she begin to explain? The differences between Kurt and her went far deeper than money. She and Kurt were all wrong for each other; they were complete opposites in interests, temperament, and methods. What sort of madness had possessed them to think their marriage could actually work?

As her mother placed a mug before her, Heather took a deep breath. "Last year at the wedding, all the signs were there. I should have seen them. I should have known we wouldn't last a year."

Mom fished a spoon out of the cluttered flatware drawer, then sent it clattering across the table toward Heather. She explored the kitchen counter for a minute, then lifted a mound of newspapers and retrieved the sugar bowl from beneath them. Her expression softened into a smile as she sank into her usual chair, the one at Heather's left hand. "Why would you say that, honey? I remember sitting at your wedding and thinking you were the most perfect couple I'd ever seen. I knew I had never seen a bride as beautiful."

"None of that matters, Mom." Heather ripped open her tea bag and unwrapped the string, dropping the bag into the steaming water. It was good to have something to do with her hands, no matter how small the task. Of course, Kurt thought she couldn't even handle hot tea properly. He had a little routine—after his tea had steeped, he settled his tea bag in the curve of his spoon, then wrapped the string around the bowl of the spoon until every blessed drop of liquid had been squeezed into the cup. His exact, precise ritual was almost feminine, but no one would dare say so in Kurt's presence. He was a brawny six-foot-two, with dark hair and startling blue eyes that could stop a woman from across a crowded room. They had certainly stopped Heather.

But she had never seen him drink hot tea before the wedding. He'd been a coffee man on those cold winter nights they dated, and he drank Diet Coke the summer before the wedding. She didn't even know he *liked* hot tea until three months after the honeymoon. It was one of the thousand things about her husband she didn't know and would never have guessed.

She used the edge of her finger to wipe tears from the wells of her eyes, then stared into her mug. "You know, I didn't even know Kurt when we got married," she said, watching as brown streamers of tea swirled in the hot water. "Do you remember when the flower girl started whining in the middle of the ceremony? I didn't even notice, but Kurt did."

"What did he tell her, anyway?" Her mother tilted her brow as she stirred her tea. "I always meant to ask you. We were all surprised when he leaned over to talk to that little girl right in the middle of the ceremony."

"He promised her a new toy if she was quiet"—Heather rubbed her temple as her head ached with the memory— "but said that if she didn't shape up he'd sit her on the front pew with Daddy."

Her mother's mouth twitched with amusement. "I always wondered how Kurt got her to behave." She brought her mug to her lips and blew on the hot liquid for a moment, then smiled at her daughter. "To be perfectly honest, I don't think anyone was paying much attention to that little girl. Most people were still thinking about how you tripped up the stairs. I don't know why you insisted on wearing those three-inch heels."

"I wanted to look him in the eye when we said our vows." Heather's throat closed as she remembered how much she had wanted Kurt to see all the love in her heart. "I—I can't talk about that now, Mom." She shook her head. "Maybe my tripping up the stairs was an omen—God's way of telling me I was about to make a mistake."

"That's sheer foolishness." Mom lowered her mug as her brown eyes brightened and filled with conviction. "Your tripping was an accident, that's all, and I think Kurt was pretty smart to threaten that fidgety flower girl with your daddy. He kept her from ruining the entire ceremony."

Heather refused to return her mother's smile. "It wouldn't matter now if it had been ruined. I should have seen the signs—they were all right before my eyes, in living color. There I stood, all teary-eyed because I was thinking about Kurt and our future life together, but all he was thinking about was how to deal with that wiggly kid."

Heather lowered her gaze to her mug. The tea was black now, probably too strong to drink. In a fit of pique, she lifted the tea bag out of the cup and dropped it, heedless of the drips, on the lime-colored place mat.

"We're so different," she whispered, staring at her distorted reflection in the dark liquid. "Our marriage was a mistake. And now I'll have to find another apartment, and somehow I'll have to find a way to keep going even though—" The tears were rolling down her face again, hot tracks of loss and regret.

"Don't be so quick to give up." Her mother's voice went soft with entreaty. Sniffling, Heather looked up, and for the first time saw a faint flicker of fear in the shadows of her mother's eyes. "Honey, think about the things that brought you together. Think about how far you've come . . . before you walk away from the man you love."

The man you love. The words hung there for a moment, almost visible in the space between them, and Heather had to acknowledge the truth. She did love Kurt. As different as they were, she had loved him since the day she first saw the Stone family at church. Kurt had been a gangly boy of thirteen, but she had seen strength in his face and intelligence in those blue eyes.

And she loved him. It was that simple. Though Heather dated a stream of boys through high school and college, no one else came close to meeting the Kurt Stone standard. So eighteen months ago, when Kurt's younger brother told Heather that Kurt would be at the Kids 'n' Toys picnic on Labor Day, she convinced her boss at the newspaper that local boy Kurt Stone, the youngest executive at Kids 'n' Toys, would be the perfect subject for a personality profile. She went to the picnic, practically made a fool of herself in an effort to simultaneously charm and impress Kurt, and managed to get a decent interview in the bargain.

For once, heaven smiled on her love life. Kurt was agonizingly slow about picking up her not-so-subtle hints, but finally he realized that she intended to be a permanent fixture in his life. He needed her . . . and she knew she could never be happy with anyone else.

And so she had walked down a flower-strewn aisle with one simple determination in her mind—she was going to love Kurt Stone with all her heart and soul. She would do anything in the world to make him happy, and he would make her happy just by being his wonderful self.

Arranging the perfect June wedding had been difficult—there were times when Heather thought it would be easier to elope and leave the haggling mothers and caterers and bridesmaids to fend for themselves—but as she stood in the back of the church and listened to the trumpeter play Pachelbel's "Canon in D Major," she knew their beautiful wedding would be worth all the stress and frustration.

Six dozen candles bathed the front of the church with a soft golden glow, and three hundred of their families' closest and dearest friends turned toward Heather as she came down the aisle. Her twenty-three-year-old brother, Billy, grinned and winked at her from the front of the church. From the front pew, Heather's mother folded her hands and leaned toward the aisle, her chin quivering.

Heather squeezed her father's arm and resisted an inexplicable urge to wave like royalty. On this one night of her life, she felt like a queen about to meet her future king. A sweet dreaming haze colored her vision as she looked down the aisle and saw her bridesmaids standing like royal ladies-in-waiting anticipating the bride's arrival.

Saving the best for last, Heather looked toward the center of the church where Kurt stood with the minister on the platform. He had clasped his hands at his waist, but she could see one leg jiggling nervously. His blue eyes were dark with emotion, and the smile on his face made her feel beautiful . . . and worth waiting for.

The walk down the aisle was over before Heather knew it. As she released her father's arm she realized that she had completely forgotten to smile at her mother as she passed the parents' pew. Mom would understand. Wasn't that what leaving and cleaving were all about?

But while she was thinking about her mother, trying to negotiate the steep steps to the platform, and looking up at Kurt, her high-heeled shoes got all tangled up in the taffeta and netting and lace beneath her voluminous wedding gown. Before she knew it, the carpeted church steps were rising up to meet her. She shrieked, certain she was going to lose a tooth or something during what was supposed to be the perfect wedding.

Amazingly, Kurt caught her. He wore that silly *you're adorable* smile as he bent down, and his hand was strong as steel around her arm. If she hadn't squealed, the people at the back of the church might never have known that she had nearly fallen flat on her face.

"Dearly beloved," the minister began. Heather breathlessly handed her bouquet to her maid of honor, then took Kurt's hands and turned to face him, only half-hearing the vows they had chosen from the minister's little black book of rituals. They had wanted a traditional service, but with a touch of modern flair. They wanted enough sentiment to make their mothers feel they were justified in wiping tears away, but not so much that their more sophisticated friends would roll their eyes. After all, Kurt had told Heather, "We aren't teenagers in the throes of puppy love. We are mature adults with established careers, and we know we'll be happier living together than living apart."

It wasn't the most romantic assertion Heather had ever heard, but it was enough.

The sound of Kurt's name brought her back to reality. "Do you, Kurtis Anthony Stone, take Heather Michelle Irvin to be your lawfully wedded wife? Do you believe God has brought you together and led you to give your lives to each other in love? Will you give yourself to helping Heather reach her full potential as a person created in God's image? Will you cherish her with tender love just as Christ loves and cherishes his bride, the church?"

Kurt's eyes glowed with the deep, clear blue that burns in the heart of a flame. "I will."

The minister turned to Heather next. "Heather Michelle Irvin, do you take Kurtis Anthony Stone to be your lawfully wedded husband? Do you believe God has brought you together and has led you to give your lives to each other in love? Will you give yourself to helping Kurt reach his full potential as a person created in God's image? Will you be faithful to him and care for him as the church is loyal to Jesus Christ?"

Heather lowered her gaze as the pastor addressed her, then she looked up at Kurt and gave him a smile straight from her heart. "I will."

The minister continued with a speech about the ring and its symbolism, and that's when the four-year-old flower girl—one of Heather's cousin's kids—began to fidget. Heather blocked the sound of the girl's whining from her mind, knowing the ceremony wouldn't last much longer, but suddenly Kurt released her hand, gestured for the minister to wait, then leaned down and whispered in the little girl's ear.

Heather stared, speechless, as the kid's eyes widened in astonishment, then the girl's lower lip edged forward in a pout. Kurt straightened, looked at the minister, and calmly said, "Go on."

Pastor Harrison didn't have to be told twice. He finished the ceremony at double speed, probably as afraid as Heather that the flower girl was on the verge of a full-blown temper tantrum. Heather and Kurt exchanged rings and lit the unity candle, they kissed, people clapped, and before Heather knew it she was Mrs. Heather Irvin Stone, a new woman with new initials—and quite delighted that they spelled HIS.

Heather blinked the images of the past away as fresh tears stung her eyes. She wouldn't be *his* much longer. This morning the stark light of reality had shone upon their lives, revealing the deep chasm between them, and Heather had never felt more convinced that she and Kurt were totally incompatible. They didn't think alike. They didn't enjoy the same things. And she had news for the guy who wrote *Men Are from Mars, Women Are from Venus.* She was from Earth, but Kurt was from somewhere beyond Pluto.

Today should have been a day of rejoicing, but never had one single morning so conclusively proven that they did not, could not, belong together.

She lowered her head onto her hand, not willing for her mother to see her tears. One year ago today she had made the worst mistake of her life, and she had no idea how to make things right again.

Chapter Two

Kurt didn't know how long he'd been running, and he didn't particularly care. This was a first. Normally he'd put in his obligatory thirty minutes of suffering then stagger up his porch, gasping for air, while all the time wondering why he subjected himself to this daily torture. Of course he knew the answer had something to do with medical benefits, though he secretly suspected they'd soon discover that exercise actually caused heart disease . . . and that the real cure for high cholesterol was fried pork rinds and Beer Nuts, digested in a sedentary position for as long as possible in front of ESPN.

It wasn't that Kurt hated running, it was just that he could think of a lot more important things to do with his time than pulling hamstrings and hitting every possible Don't Walk sign in the city.

But today the pain and inconvenience didn't bother him. Today he could have run forever. In fact, he actually took the long way and headed down State Street. He felt no fatigue, no exhaustion. Only anger. And frustration.

Insensitive? Selfish? How dare she accuse him, she, of all people! After all he'd done for her. All he'd sacrificed for her. All the times he let her have her own self-centered way, regardless of how obviously wrong it was. Kurt ran harder, already feeling the wind starting to burn the back of his throat.

He couldn't remember the first time he suspected they weren't right for each other. Maybe it was the night he proposed. That little scene had nearly ended their marriage before it began. (The State of Illinois frowns upon marrying people if one of them is deceased.)

Yes, sir, that should have been his first clue . . .

He'd spent over a month thinking up creative ways to pop the question. He'd already bought the ring, which he knew full well would be exchanged (Heather could be the picky type) and made reservations at La Traviata, which was far too expensive (but Heather was also the romantic type). Of course she would have loved for him to drop to his knee right there in front of God and everyone to ask for her hand in marriage. But each time he rehearsed the scene in his head, he saw himself breaking into laughter right at the crucial moment. No. Although some would have called it romantic, he knew she would have agreed it would have been far too corny.

He rounded State Street and jogged in place, waiting for the light to change. As he did, his thoughts drifted back to the night of the proposal. He'd worked everything out. Gone to great lengths making sure the waiter placed the ring in the bottom of the crystal goblet containing the sparkling cider served with dry ice on a fog-enshrouded tray as the band played "The First Time Ever I Saw Your Face"—an oldie but goodie they had made "their" song. If she wanted romance, she'd get romance. But, of course, everything had its price:

Twenty dollars to the waiter.

Twenty dollars to the band leader.

Twenty dollars to the maitre d'.

He had dropped sixty bucks before they'd even ordered. Not that it mattered . . . well, not much. The point was that he went to great lengths and expense, only to have Heather turn the occasion into another one of her famous fiascoes, fiascoes he often found frustrating, embarrassing, and—though he pretended to deny it—at times wonderfully endearing.

First came the toast. He'd thought she'd seen the ring. Why else would those big, beautiful brown eyes be brimming with tears . . . tears which brought a lump to his own throat. How he loved making this woman happy.

Unfortunately, that was as good as it got. In the midst of drinking the toast came the accidental swallowing of the ring. Hey, it could happen to anybody. But after that . . . after that came what could only be described as vintage Heather.

She began motioning wildly to her throat.

"Honey, what's wrong?"

More wild motioning.

"You swallowed it? You swallowed the ring?"

She shook her head.

"You didn't swallow the ring?"

More head shaking.

"I'm sorry, I don't—"

It was about this time that Kurt noticed another important fact: his bride-to-be was no longer breathing. Wheezing, yes. Gasping for air, you bet. But not exactly breathing.

"Are you choking?" He leapt to his feet, spilling the sparkling cider onto his slacks (add another $5.25 for dry cleaning). "Is that it? You're choking?"

She nodded enthusiastically, giving him a thumbs-up.

By now he was at her side. "Cough it up, hon!" he shouted, as if for some reason choking also made a person deaf. "You've got to get rid of that thing! Do you hear me, you've got to get rid of it!"

Heather stopped just long enough to give him an *I-think-I've-got-the-picture* look before going back into her coughing and gasping routine.

By now Kurt had moved behind her and lifted her to her feet. In one swift movement he placed his arms about her, doubled his two hands into a single fist, and yanked hard into her abdomen. He'd never done the Heimlich maneuver, but he'd certainly seen it enough on TV.

Writhing in his arms, Heather shook her head and grabbed his wrists.

"Don't fight me, hon!" he shouted. "We've got to get that out!" He yanked again, even harder.

More resisting and writhing.

"Higher!" the man from the next table yelled.

"What?"

A silver-haired gentleman with a matching wife motioned toward Heather. "You're pushing on her bladder. Go up higher."

Heather nodded in urgent agreement.

Never one to ignore good advice, Kurt moved his fist higher and gave another jerk.

Nothing.

Then another.

That did the trick. The ring shot out of Heather's throat like a cork from a bottle. That was the good news. Grateful for the much-needed air, she leaned over the table, panting, giving him a weak smile. More good news.

Then came the bad . . .

It seems the ring had made a perfect, full-carat landing in the silver-haired wife's platter of linguini. No problem, except for the splashing of the sauce on her slate gray chiffon dress. (Tack another $9.95 onto the dry cleaning bill.) Still no problem, except the splattering linguini so startled the woman that she reared back in her chair, nearly toppling it. Even that wouldn't have been so bad if it weren't for the waiter behind her—the one carefully balancing a tray full of the evening's specialty, some sort of eggplant parmesan with more than its fair share of tomato sauce. The eggplant parmesan and tomato sauce that flew from his tray and suddenly accessorized the evening wear of another half-dozen restaurant patrons.

Thankfully, no one was hurt, and for the most part everyone was understanding and gracious, though names and phone numbers were exchanged, just in case.

Of course, Heather and Kurt were too embarrassed to stick around and eat. So, after another round of apologies, he wrapped his arm about Heather in a gesture of solidarity and led her outside. But even as they stepped into the brisk night air he was silently tabulating the bill: $60 for additional dry cleaning, $200 to reorder ten eggplant parmesan specials, $2,950 for a ring that was somehow lost in all the commotion, and another $100 for any additional damages that may have been overlooked but which the restaurant assured them would be added to the bill.

Grand total: $3,310, without the sparkling cider. Not a bad day's work, even by Heather's standards. But one that, if he had been paying attention, should have warned him of things to come.

Kurt was wheezing harder as he rounded the corner and started up Sycamore Avenue. He allowed the memory to linger a moment longer. For as frustrating as these episodes could be, there was something about Heather's calamities that he also found touching. When they didn't infuriate him, they moved him. They revealed a tender, more vulnerable side to her, a side that always brought out the protector in him.

But there were the other times, like this morning.

Selfish? Insensitive? How dare she! After all he'd been through. After all he'd done. The anger drove him to run harder. His legs were beginning to lose feeling, but it didn't matter.

Okay, granted, maybe he'd made a mistake with the honeymoon. Maybe it hadn't been such a good idea. Maybe he should have listened to Irene and the other women in his office. But Heather loved the outdoors. And what better way for two people to really spend time together than by camping in the Alaskan wilderness? It would be a dream come true. They would fish in some of the world's most pristine streams, hike into some of the most breathtaking and remote places on earth, and sleep under the stars far from civilization, far from its superficial comforts and trappings.

All of his friends thought the idea was genius. And Heather wasn't just a friend, she was his *best* friend. She should have loved it, too.

It wasn't his fault that no one warned him about the mosquitoes. And what were the chances of nonstop rain for fourteen days, without so much as a glimmer of sunshine? She couldn't blame him for that.

Even so, he'd taken full responsibility for the honeymoon and admitted it was a mistake—one Heather had said she'd forgiven. At least that's what she'd *said*. Funny, when his guy friends forgave and forgot, things were forgiven and forgotten, but apparently that wasn't the case with Heather. The two of them could be arguing over the price of cat food and suddenly, out of the blue, she would hit him with, "Well, you're the one who dragged me up to that God-forsaken place on our honeymoon!"

It was absurd! What did honeymooning in the wilderness of Alaska have to do with the price of Kitty Kibble?

But, sure enough, she had used it on him again just this morning. All week she'd been dropping hints about their upcoming anniversary, and all week he pretended not to notice. Little did she know he'd been saving and planning for her gift for months—far longer than it took for her to throw together her little present for him.

Granted, she'd gotten the jump on him by fixing him breakfast in bed—his favorite, freshly squeezed orange juice, Swedish pancakes, and fresh-ground Amaretto coffee. And there had been nothing better than waking up and seeing her lovely face as she proudly presented the breakfast tray with an anniversary card on it. It had definitely been a Hallmark moment.

What was not a Hallmark moment was when she snuggled up next to him and accidentally spilled the freshly squeezed orange juice all over his pancakes. Fortunately, he was able to initiate damage control before the mood was entirely broken.

"No, honey," he had said after stabbing a piece of soggy dough with his fork and shoving it into his mouth. "It's really better this way. Honest. It gives it kind of, I don't know, a tropical island taste."

He didn't know if she bought it or not. Swedish tropical islands might have been a stretch, but she seemed to appreciate the effort.

However, she did not appreciate him skimming through the card.

"You barely read it," she complained after he set it down and gave her a kiss.

"Of course I did."

"Really?"

He pulled her closer and kissed her again, hoping to distract her. Funny cards he enjoyed. Brightly colored, big-gut-over-the-belt cartoon cards with one- or two-line zingers, he read. Large, pastel-and-glitter cards with dewy-eyed couples and fifty lines of "why I love you," he skimmed.

Fortunately, his diversionary tactic worked. Forgetting his blunder, she reached down and produced a large, flat package with floral wrapping.

"For me?" he asked as he began tearing aside the paper. Even then he suspected it was not the new racquetball racket he'd been so careful to ogle at in front of her. And, by the looks of things, it was definitely not that new set of graphite golf clubs he'd been mentioning. No, not this time. This time it was—

"A picture frame?" he asked, trying to sound surprised (though it really wasn't that difficult).

"Not the frame, silly. Turn it around and take a look at the front."

Kurt obeyed and flipped the thing over. In the frame before him lay a collage of at least a dozen carefully cut photographs, maybe more. There were pictures of the two of them at the lake, lounging around the house, barbecuing, visiting Six Flags. He saw romantic shots, goofy shots, candid shots, posed shots. There was even a picture of them in Alaska.

"Wow," he said. "This is, uh . . ." And that moment's hesitation was his mistake. "This is great!"

But the damage had already been done.

"You don't like it," she said.

"No, of course I do. I like it a lot." He tried to sound convincing. "There's that picture of us on the beach, and at Six Flags. Oh, and this is that photo of you and me—"

"I know what the pictures are, Kurt, I put them together. You don't like it, do you?"

"Of course I do. I think it's great, just great." He was trying too hard and he knew it. He reached over to give her another hug, but this time she wasn't buying it.

"You wanted those golf clubs, didn't you?"

"What golf clubs?" He fixed an innocent look to his face, but apparently not innocent enough.

"I spent a lot of time working on this."

"I know you did, sweetheart, and I really—"

"If you looked at it a little more closely you'd see all the detail, you'd see the way each picture captures a phase of our life while also transitioning into the next."

Kurt looked at the pictures. "Oh yes, I see it now, I see what you're talking about. The way this picture leads into the next which leads into—" His hand trailed over the photos, which ended on a Polaroid of Heather with a big, silly, red bow tied around her waist. He was about to say something about how good she looked, but he knew it was too little, too late. The battle was already over. It was time to cut his losses and move on. So he did.

Fixing her with his best mischievous grin, he said, "But it seems to me that you've missed a very important picture."

"What's that?"

"Oh, I don't know." He threw off his covers and crossed over to her side of the bed. He reached out to take her hand. "Maybe a photo of our brand new addition."

"What are you talking about?" she asked as he helped her to her feet.

He could hear the excitement in her voice as he escorted her out of the bedroom and down the hall. "Kurt—what new addition? What did you buy?"

"Oh, I don't know. What could I buy for the most gorgeous woman in the world? What could I possibly purchase to show my appreciation to her for hanging out with a slob like me?"

"Kurt, tell me." She clapped her hands together. "Don't keep me guessing!"

This was the part of her he liked the best—her little-girl excitement, her childlike enthusiasm. In her fluffy robe, tousled hair, and bunny slippers she looked just like a kid at Christmas.

"Kurt?"

They reached the front door. He said nothing, but allowed the tension to build as he fumbled to unlock the dead bolt.

"Kurt, what did you get?"

"Just a little present for the most caring and thoughtful person in the world. Just a little something to say how very,

very, much I love her." He turned the knob, stepped aside, and gave the door a push.

The anticipation on Heather's face froze. It didn't decrease, but it didn't increase, either. Maybe it was shock; maybe he'd outdone himself and simply overwhelmed her.

"A truck?" she finally asked hoarsely. "You bought me a truck?"

He laughed. "Not a truck, Heather. A brand-new, deluxe edition Toyota 4Runner."

She continued to stand in the doorway, staring.

"Come on." He wrapped an arm around her and they stepped outside. He was a little disappointed that the morning dew had dulled the deep forest green shine, but it was a minor concern. He tightened his grip around her waist. "Remember how we kept looking at those soccer mom vans? Well, this is the same, only better."

"A truck?" Heather repeated. "You bought me a truck?"

"No, that's what I'm saying, it's not a truck. It's like one of those mindless minivans you like so much, only—" That's when he turned and saw her expression.

"What's wrong?"

She shook her head.

"Don't you like it?"

"Yeah, it's—I think it's . . . great. Just great."

"You don't like it, do you?"

"Well, it's, uh—"

"What's wrong? Say it."

"Nothing."

"Heather."

"Well . . ." She swallowed. "I mean . . . it's a truck."

He could feel his excitement turning to frustration. "Why do you keep saying that?"

"Because that's what it is."

"No." He pulled her to the vehicle's front door and threw it open. "Does that look like the inside of a truck to you? Take a look at that dash. Cruise control, CD player, state-of-the-art tuner, graphic equalizer, forty-watt speakers, dual airbags, climate control, GPS navigation. No, my dear, this is anything but a truck."

"Kurt, there's no reason to get angry."

"I'm not getting angry."

"You're raising your voice."

"I am not raising—" He caught himself and tried to speak softer. "I am not raising my voice. The point is, I went to a lot of trouble to pick out the perfect gift for you."

"And I didn't?"

"Of course you did." He ran his hand through his hair, no longer able to hide his irritation. "But I've been saving for nearly nine months and this cost—"

"So it's about money?"

"I didn't say that."

"You resent my gift because I didn't spend as much!"

"I *don't* resent your gift."

"Well, you certainly weren't doing handsprings over it."

"It's just—" Kurt felt himself being sucked into an argument with little he could do to stop it.

"It's just what?" He heard the telltale tremble in her voice.

"Well, this is a substantial investment, Heather. I was hoping you might be slightly pleased."

"I didn't say I wasn't."

"Well, *you* certainly weren't doing handsprings."

"If it's such a substantial investment, why didn't you ask my opinion first?"

"I just naturally figured my judgment was good enough to—" He caught the flicker of sarcasm crossing her face. "Excuse me?"

She didn't reply.

"Do you have a problem with my judgment? Heather? Heather, answer me."

"I don't have a problem with your judgment, but . . ."

"But what?"

"Well, I'm not the one who chose Alaska for a honeymoon."

He stared at her, dumbfounded. Her chin was thrust forward and he could see the tears welling up in her eyes. Before he could respond, she pivoted on her heel and headed for the front door.

"Heather . . . Heather!"

Inside, the argument continued to escalate. Soon it all surfaced. The months of hurt, the frustration, the resentment.

"Why does your way always have to be the right way?" she demanded.

"Because I think things through and make logical decisions."

"And I don't?"

He hesitated.

Her hands went to her hips. "And I don't?"

All right, if she wanted to hear the truth, she'd hear it. "No, you don't. You leap and *then* you look. And then you expect others to clean up after you."

He could practically hear her gasp. "Is that what you've been thinking all these months?"

He said nothing.

"I can't believe it. That's so . . . unfair."

"You wanted the truth."

She began to tremble, she was so angry. But the genie was out of the bottle and there was no way of getting it back in. And, never being one to cower in the face of battle, her response was equally as biting. "Well, at least I don't think every detail to death until I've completely wrung the fun out of it and neither of us is happy."

"What?" It was Kurt's turn to reel. She spun around and started down the hall. He pursued her. "What's that mean?"

She did not respond.

"Answer me! Heather, are you telling me you're not happy?"

She turned to him, tears spilling down her cheeks. "Do I look happy?"

And still it grew. Her accusations, her anger, her resentment. And, of course it was all *his* fault; it was all due to *his* insensitivity and *his* selfishness. *His selfishness?* Well, if she wanted to fight that fight, he had more than enough ammunition stored up. When was the last time she emptied the cat box? When was the last time they'd eaten at a restaurant he wanted to eat at? When was the last time they watched a video he wanted to watch?

The gloves were off. The civilities fell. Suddenly they had become children—slamming doors, shouting at one another, voicing regrets that they'd ever met, let alone been married. So much anger, so much poison stored up and in such a short amount of time.

Eventually Heather's closet door was thrown open and an overnight bag was pulled down from the shelf.

"What are you doing?"

No answer.

"Heather, I'm asking you a question."

But she remained silent—though the tears and violent packing spoke volumes. Five minutes later she was climbing into her old Ford Escort. He didn't follow her back outside but heard the car door slam, the engine rev up, and the chirp of tires as she peeled out of the driveway.

That had been nearly ninety minutes ago.

Now, exhausted, Kurt wheezed around the final corner and started up their street. His legs had turned to rubber and he was sure his breathing had worn a groove into the back of his throat. But he kept running. He'd be home in a minute. Sweating, he'd drag himself into the shower, dry off, get dressed, and then . . . well, then he didn't know what he'd do. Maybe catch a game. Turn on some music, nice and loud. After she'd left the house it had grown so quiet so quickly. That was one of the reasons he'd gone on his run.

Then again, maybe she'd already be home. Maybe she'd seen her mistake and was ready to try and make up. Part of him hoped so. But, as the driveway came into view, there was no sign of the Escort. And despite the anger, despite the exhaustion, Kurt Stone felt his heart sink.

Chapter Three

With the same distaste with which she might have handled a dead rat, Heather picked up the soggy tea bag with two fingers, then dropped it into her empty mug. Her mother had slipped away to shower and dress, and Heather's father now stood at the kitchen counter, tapping his spoon against the sugar bowl as he waited for the coffeemaker to finish brewing his morning cup. He hadn't asked about her red-rimmed eyes, but he kept glancing at her as if she were a bomb expected to detonate at any minute.

"Is Billy home?" she asked, taking pains to keep her voice level. She wasn't sure she wanted to see her younger brother. Having never had a more serious relationship than his twenty-year infatuation with Princess Leia, he probably wouldn't understand why she was so upset.

"Billy's at that Star Trek convention in Chicago." Her father tossed the words over his shoulder, then looked at her with his eyelids lowered to cautious slits. "He'll be back tomorrow."

"Oh." Heather dabbed at her eyes with a tissue, then took a deep breath. Good. She wanted to be alone with her misery for a while; she needed time to think. Her father certainly wouldn't intrude; not once in Heather's twenty-six years had he counseled her in affairs of the heart. He would emphatically offer his opinions about cars and mortgages and politicians, but he religiously avoided any topic that might evoke a woman's tears.

The coffeemaker finally stopped sputtering. Heather said nothing as her father poured a cup of the fragrant liquid into his favorite mug. He took a seat at the table—as usual, the seat opposite her—and caught her eye for a moment before picking up the newspaper. "Don't worry, kiddo," he said, blinking. "This will blow over. These things always do."

"Thanks, Dad." Heather forced a smile, then nodded toward the family room. "I think I'll go watch the news or something."

Her father nodded in what looked like relief as Heather slipped from her chair and moved to the family room. She sank into the worn sofa and picked up the television remote, punched the power on, then stared at the screen as it filled with the images of a man and woman ecstatically promoting the advantages of the Wonder Wok, a new and improved kitchen gadget guaranteed to last twenty years without a scratch.

Heather felt the corner of her mouth droop. Unless something drastically changed, the Wonder Wok would last longer than her marriage. She and Kurt had been married for exactly twelve months, and she felt as though she had already endured a lifetime of dings and scratches.

"Darling?" Her mother called from the bathroom. "Don't forget that the cable installer is supposed to come today. If he comes while I'm in the shower, you'll have to let him in."

Her father grunted in acknowledgment, and Heather tilted her head as she listened. How in the world had her parents managed to survive almost thirty years of marriage? Frankie and Henry Irvin were very different people, but Heather had often thought that her parents could read each other's minds. They were constantly finishing each other's sentences, and they moved in sync throughout their small house, never seeming to get in each other's way.

She and Kurt, however, were forever stepping on each other's toes. After the wedding, she had been thrilled at the idea of moving into Kurt's cozy house. She had been impressed that the man even owned a house; most of her newly married friends were living in apartments or other rented housing while they struggled to scrape together a down payment on a home of their own. But responsible, practical Kurt had already bought a tidy little bungalow on a large lot, with plenty of room for expansion . . . and a family. The little house even had a guest room, where Heather set up her office.

Within a month after their return from the honeymoon, however, the house seemed to amplify their differences. On Saturday nights Kurt wanted to fill it with friends; she dreamed of romantic evenings with dinner, candles, and a rented movie in the VCR. And though Kurt had given her complete liberty to decorate and make the house her home, he couldn't hide his preferences. He liked the kitchen counter clean and bare; she wanted the toaster and blender and slow cooker within easy reach. She also wanted to display her large collection of salt-glazed pottery on the counter.

"Isn't this more logical?" he said one afternoon when she came back from the grocery store to find her stone spice jars hidden away in a cupboard. "You won't have to dust all those little lids. And I've alphabetized the spices, so when you want ginger, you know you'll find it between the dill and the nutmeg."

"I knew where the ginger was before you moved it," Heather answered, trying to smother the smoldering embers of her temper. "And let's make the kitchen my domain, okay? You can rule over the garage and the yard; I want the kitchen and my office in the guest room. Everything else can be neutral territory."

Kurt had flung up his hands and backed away. Even though that little episode was anything but a full-fledged fight, Heather had felt a little dart of defeat enter her heart. She had assumed she and Kurt would fit together seamlessly, like the sea and the shore. Her parents' marriage was like that—sometimes Mom yielded and sometimes Dad did, but they never argued and rarely voiced their differences of opinion.

How did they manage it? Had they always been a perfect match? Or was the marriage blueprint of the seventies different from the one couples followed these days?

Heather closed her eyes, blocking the sight of the Wonder Wok and the squeaky-clean smiles of the effervescent sales duo.

Some people at the newspaper office thought she was crazy for even getting married. She had hurried to the downtown office of the *Peoria Post* the day after her return from their honeymoon. Ostensibly, she needed to submit a new W–4 form in her married name, but Heather was secretly hoping she'd have a chance to show off her wedding pictures.

"Why did you want to rush into getting married?" cracked Joan Watson, the feature editor. "I'll admit that Kurt Stone is a first-class hunk, but why not just live with the guy for a while? You're a smart girl, Heather, and one day you might decide this small-time town isn't big enough for you."

"Peoria County is plenty big enough for me," Heather replied, "as long as it's big enough for Kurt. And I believe in marriage. It's God's way of putting one man and one woman together for a lifetime."

"Listen to the innocent one." A shadow of bitterness entered Joan's face. "Aw, honey, I was once young and trusting . . . but then I got over it. You will, too."

Heather hugged her wedding album to her chest, her joy deflating like a pricked balloon.

"Stop giving the girl a hard time," Nancy Wilson called from her desk. Nancy wrote the society column and had done a beautiful job of describing every carefully planned detail of the Irvin–Stone wedding. "The institution of marriage is the bedrock of our society. If Heather wants to be married, leave her alone."

"Institution—now that's the right word." Joan leaned forward on her desk and cracked her chewing gum as she looked up at Heather. "A place for confining people who are destitute, disabled, or mentally ill. If you stay married long, Heather, you may become all three."

"But I love Kurt." Heather offered the words like a futile peace offering, knowing they would mean little to Joan, who professed to love a different man every three months or so.

"Love is one thing, marriage is quite another." As Joan lifted her chin, the hard yellow glow of the overhead fluorescent lights revealed the face of a jaded, middle-aged woman. "Honey, you're a college graduate. You've got a good job. You're talented, and you have an entire future in front of you. Your life is like a well-populated city, complete and self-sufficient, and you can't build anything new in it without tearing something down. Something's going to have to give if you're going to accommodate this marriage, and I don't think you're going to enjoy the demolition process."

Caught off guard, Heather merely stared at the older woman.

Joan cracked her gum again and gave Heather a sour smile. "Let me guess what you've been doing today—going to the bank to combine your accounts, changing your name with Social Security, waiting in line at the DMV for a new license. What was yours is now his, too, right? What did you get out of this deal?"

Heather pushed aside the hearts-and-flowers words that sprang to her lips; Joan wouldn't want to hear about promises of love and commitment. "I got as much as I gave," she said, lifting her chin. "More, in fact. I am now co-owner of a darling little house on the south side of town."

Joan chuckled with a dry and cynical sound. "Sweet thing, you didn't get a house, you got a mortgage. Thirty years of indebtedness. And you'd better pray you didn't marry a stack of maxed-out credit cards. My ex took off and left me with nothing but bills. Between the lawyers and the credit agencies, I'll be paying off debts until I'm sixty."

Heather could have shouted in relief when Jack Keener, the managing editor, came around the corner. "Well, look what the wind blew in," he joked, pausing to push his glasses up from the end of his nose. "My favorite profile writer, back from the romantic beaches of the Caribbean."

"Alaska." Heather dropped her gaze. "And it wasn't all that romantic. It was two weeks of rain and kamikaze mosquitoes—"

"See there? The bloom is off the rose already," Joan quipped, turning back to her keyboard. "At least you admit it."

Heather opened her mouth to protest, but Jack interrupted. "By the way, Heather, that was a really good piece on the retiring elementary school principal. How would you like to interview an honest-to-goodness celebrity? I've heard rumors that a pitcher for the Yankees is coming to speak at the Boys Club. If you could catch him a couple of hours before he speaks, you might be able to squeeze in an interview."

"I'd love it." She flashed him a grateful smile. "I'll call the Yankees office and see if I can set up a time for the appointment. Which pitcher is it?"

"I don't know. You'll have to call the Boys Club to find out."

Someone from the next row of cubicles called out Jack's name, but Heather reached out and caught his sleeve before he could turn away. "Jack? I have a profile scheduled to appear in tomorrow's paper, and I just wanted to check something—"

Jack's mouth curled. "What's the matter, kid? Don't you trust our editing?"

"Of course, it's just—" Rattled by the pressure of several pairs of curious eyes, Heather felt herself flush. "I just wanted to be sure they got the byline right. It should say Heather Stone, not Heather Irvin."

"Good grief, girl." Joan's sharp voice sliced into the conversation. "You're taking his name professionally? Are you nuts?"

Jack nodded and pointed in Joan's direction. "She has a point, kiddo. Your readers know you as Heather Irvin. Success in the newspaper field depends upon establishing and maintaining a readership."

Heather shrugged. "I think my readers are intelligent enough to figure out that I got married."

"At least use the name Heather Irvin Stone." This from Nancy, who was apparently following the conversation from her desk. "That way you're protected. Your readers won't be able to miss the connection."

"And if you turn out to be one of the six in ten brides who don't stay married, you can drop the guy's name like a bad habit," Joan finished. Her nails clicked over the keyboard without missing a beat, and Heather wondered how the woman could write and dispense career advice at the same time. Joan might be bitter, even pessimistic, but she knew the newspaper business.

"All right." Heather had looked up at the managing editor and smiled. "Make all my future bylines Heather Irvin Stone—not because my marriage is going to fail, but because I don't want to confuse my readers."

The memory echoed in the black stillness of Heather's mind, and she couldn't help but wonder what Joan would say if she could see Heather's tear-streaked face now.

"Set your casserole in Kasbro's new Wonder Wok, set the heat dial to warm, and keep your family's dinner hot for up to an hour," the infomercial spokeswoman was saying, her gleaming smile worthy of a toothpaste commercial. "Your family will thank you when they come in, and you'll be so glad you invested in the Wonder Wok by Kasbro, the only cooking appliance guaranteed to make everyone in the family happy . . ."

Heather's gaze drifted to the silent telephone on the end table. Kurt had probably gone out for his usual Saturday morning run after their argument. He was a creature of habit, predictable and about as sensitive as a hammer. But by now he should have come home, and surely he knew where she was. Her parents lived only forty-five miles away, and she and her folks were close. So Kurt had to know she was here, and the fact that he hadn't called could only mean he was still angry.

Why should *he* be angry? *She* was the one who had been overlooked. She had spent hours designing that collage, but he had barely glanced at her card and had completely missed the point of her photo collection. Without even consulting her, he had satisfied his whim for an expensive SUV and had the gall to claim that it was a gift for her. And now, instead of calling her, he had decided to . . . well, to do whatever men found more fascinating than caring for their wives.

While she sat here and fretted over the future of their family, he was probably on the phone with one of his friends, planning an afternoon pickup game on the basketball court. Or maybe he was outside, polishing the dewdrop spots off that awful truck.

One thing was abundantly clear: on their anniversary, on the day she had planned to give him the biggest news of her life, he didn't even care to know where she was.

She bit her lip, refusing to cry again. Instead, she rummaged through a pile of papers on the coffee table until she found a pen, then jotted down the 800 number for the Kasbro sales department.

She'd show Kurt. For Christmas, if by some miracle they were still married, she'd forget about the set of new golf clubs she had on layaway and give him a Wonder Wok instead. After all, it was guaranteed to make everyone in the family happy.

Chapter Four

"'S up, Jer?"

"Hey, Stoner."

"What's happening?"

"Nothin'."

"Yeah."

"You?"

"Same."

Lying on the sofa, barefoot and in jeans, Kurt Stone gave his six-foot-two-inch frame a stretch and did his best to sound bored. He was in his guy talk mode—that special form of communication involving as few syllables as possible while giving the impression that you have accidentally picked up the phone, dialed the other party's number by chance, and have nothing whatsoever to say. As a junior executive of an up-and-coming toy company, Kurt possessed top-of-the-line communication skills, but when it came to talking to his old college buddies, he became as monosyllabic as a teen forced to stay home Friday night and eat dinner with his parents.

It had been less than an hour since he'd run and showered. By rights, he should be tired, and he was. But not as tired as he was hurt. And angry. And lonesome. He had no idea how big their tiny house could become without Heather's presence. It didn't used to be that way, before they started dating. He had lived here for nearly two years on his own, relishing the solitude and enjoying the early morning stillness.

But now . . . now the house seemed gigantic. And as the morning dragged on, it grew bigger by the minute. How quickly she had filled it with her presence. And, like the house, how quickly she had filled his heart, a heart he hadn't even known was empty.

"Any racquetball in our future?" he asked Jerry.

"When?"

"Noonish?"

"It's Saturday."

"And?"

"Well, Bev and I, we're still fixing up the apartment. She's got me putting together one of those closet organizer thingies with her."

"Ah." Kurt did his best not to sound disappointed, but this was his second call to a friend with nearly identical results.

"Why didn't you warn me?" Jerry asked.

"'Bout what?"

Jerry's voice lowered. "She acts like I don't know the first thing about building. She's got the tools all laid out, she's got each group of screws in their own separate little pile, and get this . . ." He dropped his voice even lower. "She's got me following the instructions step-by-step like they're the Holy Bible or something."

Kurt couldn't help laughing. Jerry had only been married six, maybe seven weeks. As the last of the gang to finally "fall," the poor guy was now in the middle of the initiation process.

"I don't know how you do it," Jerry confided.

"What's that?"

"You and Heather working together on that addition. We can't even build this closet thing, and you guys are adding on a whole room?"

Kurt threw a look to the sheet of plastic hanging over the doorway past the kitchen. The sheet of plastic that had been hanging there ever since Heather had convinced him they needed to start remodeling the master bedroom. The sheet of plastic that had been hanging there just slightly short of forever. "It's all a matter of attitude," he answered.

"How's that?"

"You should be looking upon this as an opportunity."

"To . . ."

"To get in touch with your feminine side."

"Thanks, pal."

"Don't mention it. So we'll take a rain check on racquetball?"

"Yeah."

Beverly's voice echoed in the background. "Hang on," Jerry said. There was more muffled talking, then, "Stoner?"

"Yeah?"

"Now that we've got most of the boxes unpacked, Bev's thinking we should have you and Heather over here for dinner."

"Cool."

There was more background talking, and again Jerry asked Kurt to hang on. Finally, he came back. "Kurt?"

"Present."

"How 'bout a week from Saturday?"

"Sounds good to—"

"Just a minute." More talking. Finally: "Bev wonders if Heather will bring some sort of fruit salad that she makes?"

"Sure."

"Hang on." There was no missing the growing frustration in Jerry's voice, and Kurt couldn't help but smile. The two of them had been on the phone a couple minutes now, and over half that time had been devoted to Jerry and Beverly's conversation. Yes, sir, Jerry was definitely getting initiated.

"Listen, can Bev talk to Heather a sec?"

"She's not here."

More muffled talking, then Jerry came back. This time a trace of weariness accompanied his frustration. "Maybe it'd be better if we let the girls set this thing up."

"Always is," Kurt said with amusement.

"So Heather will call Bev?"

"Sure."

"And we'll do racquetball soon."

"Deal."

With that they hung up. No "good-byes," no "see yas," just a brisk disconnection—Jerry's obvious attempt to salvage his manhood by returning to their testosterone communication technique.

Kurt glanced down at the address book resting on his chest. There was still one call he could make. Though it was to a friend he didn't relish calling . . .

Charlie.

Of the old group, Charlie was always the most available. Anytime you wanted to do something, Charlie was there. That was the up side of his friendship. But there was also a down side. Charlie was divorced.

Actually, the divorce wasn't the problem. It was what the divorce was doing to him. Eating away at him. Making him angry. Oh, he still had the old Charlie wit, the smart mouth that nearly got them beaten up by a couple of college football linemen their sophomore year. But now that humor was turning in upon itself, becoming bitter, biting.

Then there was his womanizing. Charlie's hunger had become insatiable. His conquests—at least according to Charlie—were innumerable. He was like an alcoholic, only instead of booze it was women. Kurt and Heather knew that if the poor guy didn't get help, he'd eventually destroy himself. That's why they'd been praying for him. And that's why, despite Charlie's refusals and put-downs, Kurt continually invited him to his men's group at church.

Kurt stared at the address book a long moment, then snapped it shut and tossed it on the coffee table. Racquetball on his anniversary? Was he nuts? This was their day, his and Heather's. He had blocked out this Saturday in his day planner months ago. He'd made sure there would be absolutely no interruptions. He even left the laptop at the office, in case the temptation to work should arise.

But now . . .

He looked at his watch. It was almost noon. Where was she? He rose, strode into the kitchen, and grabbed a Diet Coke from the fridge. Once again the silence of the house loomed around him. Everything was so empty, so vacant.

Dinner was in seven hours. At La Traviata. He'd heard there had been a large turnover in the help, which would decrease their chances of being recognized. And since there would be no exchange of gifts or other life-threatening objects, he figured it would be as safe as any other place to dine.

Realizing he hadn't shaved and that this would be an effective use of this down time (even on his days off Kurt prided himself on efficient time management), he pushed through the sheet of plastic and headed into the bathroom.

Ah, the bathroom. If ever there was a space that proved their incompatibility, it was this tiny little room. Initially they had worked out the basics. As an early riser, Kurt showered first, then scooted out as quickly as possible so Heather could have the rest of the morning to do her makeup and all that other girl stuff.

No problem.

He'd also adjusted to the other bathroom deportment such as cleaning the mirror after flossing, rinsing the sink after shaving, and, of course, the ever-important closing of the toilet seat.

No problem.

But when it came to the medicine cabinet . . . well, that was a problem.

"I've got it all worked out." Heather had beamed the day she unloaded her crates of makeup, makeup remover, fingernail polish, nail polish remover, and all other manner of cosmetics and cosmetic removers—each in a tiny, odd-shaped container that took up three times the space of a regular container while holding half the amount of stuff. "You can take the top three shelves," she said, "and I'll have the bottom four."

Kurt laughed. "Sweetheart, there's no way you can get all that stuff into one medicine cabinet."

She rose up on her toes to give him a kiss. "Sure I can."

"But—the laws of physics—it's not possible."

"Just leave everything to me," she said, ushering him out of the room.

And, sure enough, half an hour later Kurt realized that the laws of physics were no match for female ingenuity. When he returned, the bathroom was spotless, and everything was in its place. He looked at the closed door of the medicine cabinet with fear and trepidation. Dare he open it? He'd once made that mistake when visiting her apartment, only it pertained to her coat closet. He hadn't been badly injured, but it had taken a few minutes to dig him out.

It's not that Heather was a bad housekeeper, it was just that . . . well, all right, she was a bad housekeeper. Terrible.

But that didn't diminish his love for her, or his respect. So what if she gave new meaning to the phrase *random chaos?* It was just another one of those endearing idiosyncrasies that had captured his heart. Besides, organization was not a hard skill to teach. And until she was able to grasp it, he could learn to adjust.

Yet, when he had reached over and opened the medicine cabinet that very first time, he was astonished. Stunned. Each and every shelf had been cleaned and arranged as neatly as a GI's footlocker. Her bottles, jars, and whatevers were stacked perfectly and efficiently, filling her four shelves and not an inch more. It was an amazing feat, a remarkable accomplishment. And if she could manage this on her own, imagine what she could accomplish with just a little of his tutoring.

But that had been a year ago. And today . . .

Today Kurt opened the cabinet with his right hand while instinctively cupping his left to catch whatever would spill out. Although every morning brought a new frustration, he had to admit it was a great way of maintaining his hand-eye coordination. As a matter of fact, in the last six months they had suffered only two casualties—a jar of moisturizing cream that had slipped through his fingers to shatter on the tile counter, and that unfortunate bottle of fingernail polish remover. He'd nearly caught it twice, but his juggling only managed to bounce it over to the shower stall, where the top came off and it spilled, eating a hole the size of Detroit in the shower's fiberglass floor.

But today there were no surprises. Just the usual search and rescue for his razor.

As the days of their marriage turned into weeks and the weeks into months, Heather's things slowly began to encroach upon his space. But Kurt was understanding. Although he assured her a hundred times that she didn't need any of that beauty stuff, that she still took his breath away whenever he saw her walk into a room, and that he still stared at her sleeping profile to marvel over her beauty, nothing he said made any difference. For some reason Heather always thought she was seven pounds too heavy and that she really needed all that junk to make her attractive. So, always a good sport, he let her have an extra shelf . . . then two . . . then three. It was only when it took half an hour to find his razor that Kurt got a little testy.

Where was it? Where was that stupid razor? He'd put it in the medicine cabinet just yesterday. He pushed bottles back and forth on the bottom shelf, clanking them into each other just a little harder than necessary as his frustration rose. That was his razor, wasn't it? Surely, he was entitled to use his razor when he wanted. That wasn't too much to ask, was it?

The anger increased as he finished searching the first shelf. This was so typical. It was never the big things she did that annoyed him, just the little things.

There was nothing on the first shelf. He started on the second. It wasn't like she did this on purpose, he knew that. But that didn't make it any less of an inconvenience.

Nothing on the second. He started the third. What was wrong with offering him a little common respect and courtesy? What was wrong with giving him a call to at least let him know where she was?

He moved to the fourth shelf. But wasn't this typical of their entire marriage? One compromise after another—giving up this thing and that thing until finally whatever rights he had were completely taken? No doubt Heather had given up some things, too, but at the moment he was hard-pressed to remember any.

The fifth and sixth shelves offered the same lack of success, though he was grateful to find the mint floss that he'd thought had been forever lost.

When had it started, this perpetual giving up? Giving up his house. Giving up his space. Giving up his time. Here he'd sacrificed an entire Saturday to spend with his wife, and she'd just blown it off with the same thoughtless abandon that she took everything else of his—including that stupid razor!

The search of the seventh shelf was equally fruitless. He slammed shut the cabinet. Where could it be? Where could she have possibly put—

Wait a minute. The shower. He'd asked her a dozen times not to use his razor and a dozen times she had apologized with some excuse. He reached for the door and slid it open. Sure enough, there on the shelf, surrounded by all manner of shampoos, body bars, and conditioners, lay his shaver.

That was the last straw. He'd had enough. She could have his bathroom, she could have his shelves, she could even have his razor, but she couldn't have his life. Not all of it. No. Right now he wanted to play racquetball, and right now racquetball was what he would play!

He stormed out of the bathroom, pushed through the plastic, and stalked into the overcrowded guest room/office where they'd been sleeping since the remodeling began. He opened his dresser drawer and rummaged around for a pair of sweat socks. He found nothing but a few mismatched black and brown dress ones. Of course. After all, the laundry was one of Heather's jobs. It didn't have to be that way; he'd offered more than once to split the laundry chores, but she always took it as an affront to her womanhood, as if it somehow made her less of a—

Wait a minute, there was a pair of white sweat socks in the back. He grabbed them and headed for the chair. Only when he arrived did he discover that he'd grabbed a pair of Heather's white footies—the ones with the trim around the tops.

Kurt stared at them in frustration. He had three choices: dig out some smelly, dirty socks from the hamper, go with the mismatched nylon ones, or stay with the thick white cotton footies. He sighed deeply, then opted for the footies. He'd probably stretch them out, but that couldn't be helped. And it wasn't like anybody at the club would see the trim; he'd be sure to wear his sweatpants over them.

Two minutes later he was on the phone with Charlie.

"Sounds good to me," Charlie said. "I'll see you at the club in twenty."

Kurt grabbed his racket bag out of the closet and headed through the kitchen toward the door. He hesitated at the cluttered counter, wondering if he should leave a note. Then again, Heather hadn't offered him the courtesy of calling to let him know where she was, so he was certainly entitled to return the favor, wasn't he? He couldn't be blamed for that.

Come to think of it, he couldn't be blamed for any of this.

Chapter Five

By twelve-fifteen, Heather was ready to offer a truce. Her initial anger had faded, and only sheer stubbornness kept her from running to the phone and calling Kurt. She forced herself to wait, though, and quietly ate lunch with her parents. Nodding gamely to her dad's ranting about his HMO, she forced down a dry turkey-and-mayonnaise sandwich and kept her head tilted toward the family room in case the telephone should ring.

By twelve-thirty, Kurt hadn't called. While her parents laughed a little too brightly about a funny movie they'd seen last week, Heather slipped from the kitchen and hurried to the family room, then picked up the phone and dialed her number.

The phone rang in her ear. Kurt was probably sitting on his stool at the kitchen bar, munching on potato chips or polishing off the gargantuan sub sandwich he'd begun the night before. Maybe he'd been worried about her, so he'd pick up the phone as soon as it began to ring . . .

Heather pressed her lips together as the phone rang again. So—he wanted to teach her a lesson. He wanted her to be good and worried about him, then he'd pick up the phone and recite his list of Reasons Why a Wife Shouldn't Leave the House Without First Explaining Where and Why She Was Going. Honestly, the man created a list for everything. He couldn't go to the grocery store without one, and she doubted if he had ever made an impulse purchase in his life. He never did anything without a Plan A and a backup Plan B, so nothing in him would be able to understand why she had to simply get away this morning.

The phone rang a third time, then the answering machine clicked on. Heather closed her eyes as her own voice filled her ears. *Hello, you've reached Heather and Kurt, but we're not here.* The mechanical Heather laughed, for Kurt had reached out to tickle her ribs as she was recording the message. *Leave your name and number and we'll*—giggle—*we'll get right back to you . . . if we can.* More laughter, his and hers all mingled together, then the beep.

Heather hesitated for a moment. "Kurt, if you're there, will you please pick up?" She waited, but heard nothing but the hiss of the telephone line. Where was he? He could have been out in the garage, but he would have come in when he heard the phone ring. And he had no plans for the day; he had told her several times that he had purposely kept the day free for her, for their anniversary. So if he wasn't in the garage, he had to be in the house.

"Kurt?" She heard a note of desperation in her voice as fearsome images filled her head. What if he had slipped in the shower after his run? He could be lying in the shower stall right now, his head cracked open and his life's blood slowly seeping down the drain. "Honey, are you there?"

Still no answer. Fighting a rise of blind panic, Heather hung up and dialed the number of the elderly couple who lived next door. Mr. and Mrs. Scarborough were nice folks, even though they did seem extraordinarily interested in the comings and goings of the newlyweds next door. Heather and Kurt often joked about the older couple's curiosity, but today Heather would be grateful if the Scarboroughs were home and watching the house. Perhaps one of them would go over and check on Kurt.

"Hello?"

Heather sighed in relief when she heard Edith's quavering voice. "Mrs. Scarborough, this is Heather Stone, from next door—"

"Why, Heather! So nice to hear from you. I was just telling Edgar that we hadn't seen you all morning."

"Mrs. Scarborough, I'm not home, and I'm worried about Kurt. I'm sure he's at the house, but he won't answer the phone. I wonder if—"

"Your husband? Home? I don't think so, dear. Edgar saw him leave in that fancy new truck just a few minutes ago. Say, that's a beautiful vehicle. Edgar was downright jealous when he saw your handsome husband behind that wheel. Why, he looked as proud as a father with a new baby."

Disappointment struck Heather like a blow in the stomach. Kurt wasn't hurt; he was out joyriding in his new truck! She had to swallow twice before she could speak. "Thanks, Mrs. Scarborough. I'll see you later."

She lowered the phone, her heart pounding as her indignation grew. What a fool she was, thinking that Kurt needed her, missed her! He wasn't missing her at all; he was out showing off his truck in front of his friends! Well, she knew his friends, and she knew just where to catch him.

Without pausing, she dialed Jerry's number. The phone rang only once, then Bev picked up. "Hello?"

"Bev, it's Heather. Is—"

"Heather! Boy, that was quick. I thought for sure Kurt would forget to tell you."

Heather blinked and turned toward the window. "Tell me what?"

Bev laughed. "Men. I should have known he'd forget. Jerry and I want you and Kurt to come over for dinner next weekend. And if you don't mind, I'd love you to bring that delicious fruit salad you're famous for—you know, the one with the mandarin oranges."

"Okay." Heather twisted the telephone cord around her wrist. "By the way, Bev, is Kurt there? I'd like to speak to him."

"Kurt? No, honey, I haven't seen him. He called earlier to ask if Jerry could play racquetball this afternoon, but Jerry's helping me with the closet shelving."

"I see." Heather couldn't keep the frostiness out of her voice.

Bev hesitated a moment, and Heather could almost see her blue eyes widening in concern. "What's wrong, Heather? You sound a little stressed."

"We had a fight." Heather looked at the ceiling and forbade herself to cry. Kurt was not only alive and well, but he was out playing racquetball. He wasn't driving and thinking about their disagreement, or even showing off his car, but he was playing his favorite sport. Having fun. While she sat alone in tears.

"Our fight was a pretty big one," she said when she could force words over the lump in her throat. "I'm surprised he didn't mention it to Jerry."

Beverly made quiet *tsking* sounds. "No, he didn't. But if that bozo shows his face around here, I'll send him home right away. You hang in there, Heather. Things are never as serious as they seem when you're in the thick of the trouble."

"This is the biggest trouble ever." Heather sniffed, then wiped a few hot tears from the corners of her eyes. "The little things have all built up into one big mess. And you can send Kurt home if you want to, but I'm at my parents' house."

"Can I do anything?"

Heather shrugged. "You could pray. If we get through this, it'll be nothing short of a miracle."

"Aw, Heather, you can't mean that."

"I do." Heather sniffed again as the tears began to flow in earnest. "Don't let us discourage you, Bev; you and Jerry are a great couple. But I can tell you that romantic love can dry

63

up real quick, and then you look at the person you married and wonder whatever possessed you to hand your life over to a total stranger. I'm at that point right now, and I don't know how we're going to get through this."

"Then I'll be praying."

Heather hung up the phone and sat on the sofa for a long minute, one hand on the telephone. Kurt had some nerve. The man who had promised to love her through better or worse had walked out in the middle of the worst and gone to play around at the gym.

A chiding voice reminded her that she had walked out, too, but Heather shook her head, too angry to care. She didn't want to cut Kurt any slack, not today. He didn't even deserve to know that she had called and nearly panicked when he didn't pick up the phone.

Quickly, she dialed her house again, tapped her fingers against the phone as that silly recording replayed, then keyed in the special code that allowed her to retrieve messages. When she came to her own message, she hastily punched in the code again.

"I will delete the message," the robotic voice said. "Message deleted."

Heather hung up the phone, then wrapped her arms around herself and wondered why she didn't feel a sense of satisfaction.

Chapter Six

"Nice socks."

"Thanks," Kurt said as he reentered the racquetball court after taking off his sweats. "I wore them just for you."

"Really?" Charlie moved to center court, preparing to receive Kurt's serve. "Next time will you wear the ones with those furry pink balls on the heel? You know they're my favorite."

"Got it," Kurt said, bouncing the ball a couple of times and crouching to serve. "Zero games to three. Zero-zero."

The two of them had been playing forty minutes. Well, actually, Charlie had been playing forty minutes. Kurt had been giving a miserable imitation of it. Maybe it was because he was already exhausted, or maybe it was because his mind was back at the empty house. He suspected the latter. Whatever the reason, after losing the third game, four to twenty-one, he had taken a break to peel off his sweats and strip down to fighting weight.

He bounced the ball a third time, leaned back, and smashed his racket into it with all his strength . . . and all his anger. The ball slammed into the wall low and hard. It came back, smoking past Charlie so fast that, despite his lunge, he missed it by a good six inches.

Charlie whistled softly. "Where have you been hiding that one?"

Kurt smiled ruefully. Releasing the anger felt good, but even now he could feel the strain in his service arm and knew he'd be regretting it tomorrow. He scooped up the ball, gave it his standard two bounces, and announced the score, "One–zero." He bounced it a third time and attempted a repeat performance of the serve. This time, however, Charlie was ready for it. With equal speed he returned the ball and left Kurt standing flat-footed.

They switched places and Charlie served. Immediately he began racking up points. "One–one." "Two–one." "Three–one."

The carnage continued. In normal circumstances Charlie and Kurt were equally matched, but this afternoon, no matter how hard Kurt tried, he could not focus on the game. If he wasn't thinking about Heather or worrying about her, he was stewing over how radically his life had changed because of her. And we're not just talking the hogging of medicine cabinets, or playing hide-and-seek with shavers. As far as Kurt was concerned, he was talking everything.

From how he slept, to how he ate, to how (and if) he shaved, to how he worked, to how he played. He'd always expected marriage to add to his life, not take from it. But taking was all Heather ever seemed to do. Not that she did it on purpose—she was an incredibly giving person. That was one of the traits he so admired in her. But there didn't seem to be a single area of his life she had not infiltrated, that he had not given up or adjusted to suit her. Was that all marriage was? Just giving and giving and giving some more? Shouldn't he be getting something in return?

"Seven–one." Charlie's voice interrupted his thoughts. "Come on, buddy, try to at least pretend you're playing."

Kurt crouched low and focused back on the service wall. Suddenly, he remembered. There was something he had received from the marriage. Of course, how could he forget? There were his eccentric, some would say flat-out nutcase, in-laws.

Where to begin? First there was "Dad." Kurt didn't mean to be disrespectful, but the guy's outspoken opinions and narrow-mindedness made Archie Bunker seem like a card-carrying member of the American Civil Liberties Union. If there was any topic the man did not have an opinion on, Kurt hadn't discovered it. Watching the news with him was impossible. Actually, watching it was okay; trying to listen to it was the problem. Did the man really think the reporters could hear him shouting back at them? Did he really think he could carry on arguments with them?

Then there was little brother, Billy. At age twenty-four, they were still calling him "Billy." Kurt knew some guys took longer to find themselves than others, but Billy, who had quit college at nineteen, was still unemployed, still living at home, and still being waited on hand and foot by his mother.

Ah, Mom. Here was at least one member of the family who was fairly normal. A trait, that for the most part, seemed to have been passed on to the female side of the family.

He would never forget last New Year's Day. Heather thought it would be great to have "the men" of her family come over and join Kurt in his annual bowl game marathon. The Rose Bowl, the Sugar Bowl, the Hula Bowl—you name it, if it had Bowl after it, Kurt watched it. He'd relished this day since he was a kid. That's why, in an effort to integrate the families, Heather thought it would be great fun to have Dad and Billy over. And, since Gramps liked sports, too, why not bring him over from the nursing home? As always, her intentions were sweet and innocent. But, as always, the results were disastrous.

First, there were Gramps's complaints about the voices coming from the electrical wall outlets. Did Kurt really expect him to sit there while those pesky extraterrestrials kept on yacking at him during the game?

Then there were Dad's shouting matches with the referees. "I saw that! Don't think I didn't see that! Did you see where the ref moved that ball?"

Apparently everyone else was familiar with Dad's "interactive style" of television viewing and everyone else ignored him. Well, everyone but Kurt. Being uninitiated, and trying his best to be a polite host, Kurt felt it was his duty to respond. "What's that, Dad?"

"He put that ball back three yards behind the line of scrimmage!"

Kurt threw a glance to the TV, then cleared his throat. "You, uh . . . you really think so?"

"Think so? I know so! Didn't you see it?"

"Well, I, uh—"

"They always do it in these tournament games. The refs, they're all owned by the Trilateral Commission, and if the school doesn't pay protection money, well, you see for yourself what happens."

Kurt looked to the others, wondering if he'd heard correctly. No one seemed to notice. Mom had just finished refilling the chip bowl and was heading back to join Heather in the kitchen, Gramps was hunched over one of the outlets listening to alien messages, and Billy—well, Billy was busy teasing Muttley, his overfed rottweiler, which he insisted on bringing wherever he went. "Here, girl, go fetch the remote! Here, girl!"

Of course Kurt knew Billy wouldn't actually throw the TV remote—at least he hoped he wouldn't. But Muttley didn't, which would explain her leaping into Billy's lap (all ninety-six pounds of her) as she tried to grab it from his hand.

"Pass interference?" Dad yelled. "You're nuts! Get that ref a Seeing Eye dog!"

Kurt had been so distracted by Muttley and the close proximity of the animal's claws to the new $750 leather sofa that he hadn't even seen the play.

"What?" Gramps yelled at the outlet. "You've got Lawrence Welk and you're holding him hostage?"

"No, girl, let go!"

Kurt turned to see that Muttley had clamped her saber-toothed jaws around the remote and was trying to pull it from Billy.

"Morons! You commentators are all morons!"

"Muttley, let go! Let go, girl!"

Kurt's eyes darted to the big dog's claws.

"You've got Glenn Miller, too?"

"Rigged! Can't you idiots see it's all—"

"Muttley, let—"

Just then one of Muttley's teeth hit a remote button. Suddenly they were all watching the Disney Channel, the original *Parent Trap*, as Haley Mills sang, "Let's get together, yeah, yeah, yeah . . ."

"What about Benny Goodman, is he also—"

"Billy, turn it back! Turn it back!"

"I'm trying, but Muttley won't—"

"Why don't you and I com-bi-ine . . ." Haley sang on, oblivious.

"Billy!"

"Let go, girl! Let—"

"Artie Shaw?"

"How can I hear the moron commentators if you—"

"Let's get together . . ."

"Muttley! Let . . . GO!"

Suddenly Muttley tore the remote out of Billy's hands. She

leaped off the sofa, her ninety-six pounds driving her claws deep into the leather, and began racing around the room.

Billy was on his feet, after her. "Muttley, come here, girl, come here!"

But, of course, the dog saw it as a great game and barked all the louder.

"Muttley!"

"Idiots!" Dad shouted. "I'm surrounded by idiots."

"Barry Manilow?" Gramps shook his head. "I don't know a Barry Manilow."

"Muttley, I'm not kidding!"

By now all Kurt could do was stare as Billy and Muttley raced around the room, as Dad kept shouting his complaints, as Gramps continued his cosmic communications, and as Haley Mills continued to sing.

He slowly sank back into his chair. With any luck, the remote would be back before halftime. He could only pray. Just as he would certainly pray that when he and his beloved decided to have children, none of this would be genetic.

"Hey, Stoner, we got company."

Kurt glanced up and saw Charlie gesturing toward two attractive ladies taking a seat behind the glass wall, waiting for their turn on the court. One was a well-endowed blonde who gave new meaning to the word *voluptuous*. The other was a sultry-looking brunette.

"It's twenty to one," Charlie said. "We got one point left in the game. Think you can make it look like we know what we're doing?"

"I'll give it a shot," Kurt mumbled as he took his position to receive the serve. He wasn't sure if the women were watching, but he suspected so . . . which explained why he caught himself sucking in his gut. The move wasn't intentional, it was more a conditioned reflex, a way of putting his most manly foot forward. Unfortunately, that's when he glanced down and realized both feet might be a bit more manly if they weren't adorned in lace-trimmed footies.

Charlie finished him off with a powerful serve, more for the ladies' benefit than for his. And before Kurt knew it, he and Charlie were heading out the door to retrieve their stuff behind the glass wall.

"Good afternoon, ladies," Charlie said, flashing his killer grin.

"Hey." The blonde nodded. "That's some serve you've got."

"That?" Charlie shook his head. "You should see it when I'm having a good day."

Kurt busied himself unzipping his gym bag as the dance began.

"Well, it looked pretty powerful from where we sat," the blonde said.

"Actually, it's not so much a power thing as it is timing."

"Timing?"

"Yeah, it's all a matter of knowing when to snap the wrist."

"Snap the wrist?" she asked. "I thought you had to keep your wrist stiff."

"No, that's tennis. In racquetball you get the power with a last-minute snap." He demonstrated with a slow-motion swing. "See? And then at the last minute . . . *snap.*"

"Hm, I didn't know that."

Oh brother, Kurt thought. *Here we go again.* As Charlie and the blonde talked he found it odd the other woman didn't participate, until he glanced up to see her staring at him. She pretended to be embarrassed and looked away, but the look was a full-on flirt, no doubt about it. And she was gorgeous enough to get away with it—slender body, dark auburn hair, definitely in shape. In fact she was in very, very good—

Hold it! He chided himself. *You're a married man. Knock it off!*

He turned back to his gym bag and pulled off his Velcro wristband. The brunette also pretended to busy herself, but the message had been sent—and received. For Kurt the tension grew palpable. He tried to focus on Charlie's conversation. The guy was definitely making progress.

"So you used to give lessons?" the blonde asked.

"Back when I played professionally, yeah."

Played professionally? Tell me she's not buying that?

"You were a pro?"

"Well, yeah. But that was a long time ago. Now I like to play and give lessons, you know, just for the fun of it."

Kurt almost groaned. The manure was definitely getting deep.

"No kidding?" she said.

Stand by, here it comes . . .

"Sure," Charlie said. "I mean helping others—that's what life's all about, isn't it?"

She nodded. Then after a moment added, "Maybe sometime, if it's not a bother, maybe you could give Sheryl and me some pointers?"

"Sure." Charlie grinned and turned to pack his gym bag. "Sometime."

Kurt almost smiled. Now it was time for the mandatory pause, those few seconds of making her think he'd lost interest before returning to set the hook.

T-minus three seconds and counting. Two. One. And . . .

"Actually . . ." Charlie looked up from his bag. "I don't know what your schedule is like today, but I have a little time now, if you're interested."

"You do?"

Roger, Houston, we have ignition.

"Sure. In fact, if you want, the four of us could play some doubles. That way I could check out your style and give you both a few pointers."

"Sounds good to me." The blonde turned to her friend. "Pointers from a professional. What do you think, Sheryl?"

Only then did the brunette look up from her gym bag. She glanced first at her friend, then at Charlie, then locked her dark eyes onto Kurt's. "We certainly wouldn't want to be an imposition."

For a moment Kurt forgot to breathe.

"Oh, no." Charlie quickly stepped in. "No imposition at all. In fact, Kurt and I were just going out for a bite to eat.

But we could hang here and play a game or two with you first. Isn't that right, Stoner?"

All eyes turned to Kurt. Suddenly he was feeling very tense . . . and very uneasy. Why? What was so terrible about playing an extra game or two? It's not like he would be doing anything wrong. It was just a harmless game. Heather wouldn't care . . . if he ever told her. But why wouldn't he tell her?

He looked back to the woman who kept her gaze fixed on his. She really was stunning. And an extra game or two would certainly help pass the afternoon—an afternoon he had set aside for Heather, but one that she obviously didn't care to spend with him. One that she had actually thrown back into his face. But here . . . here were people interested in his time. Not only interested, but *very* interested.

What are you doing? Stop it!

But it's just a game. Just an innocent game of racquetball. What would be so wrong with—

"So, what do you say, Kurt?"

The sound of Charlie's voice brought Kurt back to reality. What was he thinking? What was he doing? Regardless of his and Heather's troubles, regardless of their differences, Kurt loved his wife. More importantly, he honored her. And no incredible figure, no smoldering dark eyes, and no "innocent game of racquetball," was going to distract him from that.

He smiled politely and shook his head. "I don't think so."

"Come on." Charlie pressed him with hard eye contact. "Just a couple of games."

"Sorry . . ." His voice was a little raspy and he cleared it. "My wife is waiting for me back home."

Suddenly the tension broke, the moment passed. By mentioning Heather he'd redefined the parameters.

"Okay, how 'bout one game?" Charlie asked.

"Sorry, guys." Kurt scooped up his gym bag and turned for the door. "I've got to get going."

He knew Charlie would remain behind and try to pick up the pieces. And he knew that later he'd get an earful of lecture over the phone. But right now it was important he ride his resistance and exit as quickly as possible.

He headed down the hall and out into the lobby. A moment later he pushed open the double glass doors and stepped into the parking lot. He stood a moment, taking a long breath of the sultry summer air.

The confrontation had taken more out of him than he had thought. Not only did it leave him a little shaken, it left him a lot concerned. He'd passed the test, sure. But why had it even been a test? What was going on?

Angry with himself, he shook his head and started toward the Toyota 4Runner. And that business about Heather waiting for him? Was he so desperate that he had to lie to get out of there? Then again, maybe it wasn't a lie. Maybe she really would be there waiting for him. He certainly hoped so. And as he slid into the car and turned on the ignition, that's what he quietly prayed for.

Chapter Seven

By one-thirty, a worried crease had settled in the center of Heather's mother's forehead. "Honey, don't you think you should at least call Kurt?" she asked, coming into the family room where Heather sat morosely on the sofa. "He's bound to be worried about you."

"He's out playing racquetball." Heather's voice sounded flat and lifeless in her own ears. "He probably hasn't thought about me in the last three hours."

"That's ridiculous, sweetheart." Mom dropped onto the end of the sofa and gave Heather a look of patient understanding. "Kurt loves you, and you know it. So give the man a call. Don't be afraid to make the first move."

"I already tried to, Mom." A flash of loneliness stabbed at Heather, and for the first time she seriously wondered if things had gone too far. "I tried to call him, but he wasn't home. I tried to track him down, and found out that he was playing racquetball. If Kurt wanted to reach me, all he had to do was call here. Where else would I go?"

"You're an independent woman, you could have gone anywhere." Settling back against the couch cushions, Mom tucked her chubby pink legs beneath her flowered housedress and regarded Heather with a level gaze. "Honey, you can't expect your husband to read your mind. Men and women are wired differently. We don't think alike."

"But he knows me better than anyone on earth! He should know where I'd go, what I'd do, and what I want." Heather raked her hand through her hair in frustration. "Do you know what he got me for our anniversary? A truck. A huge, dark, loud Something Runner. It's got every bell and whistle known to man, but I know Kurt just got it for himself. I'd have been happy with a card, roses, and chocolate."

Mom took a deep breath and adjusted her smile. "You have to give him an A for effort, Heather. A truck isn't cheap, and your car has nearly 100,000 miles on it."

"I don't care how much he spent, it's the thought that counts most, isn't it? But he didn't give me a single thought, he only wanted some macho monster machine. Sometimes he can be as thick as a plank. I don't know how such an intelligent, capable man can be so thoughtless."

"Do you love him, Heather?"

The question caught Heather off-guard. Love? For an instant her brain filled with the image of a strutting Tina Turner singing, "What's love got to do with it?" then she closed her eyes. "Of course I love him. I always will. It's just that I thought we were the perfect couple, best friends, so our marriage would be nothing but smooth sailing. I told God

I'd sacrifice anything to spend the rest of my life with Kurt, and now I feel like he's saying, 'Prove it.'"

Heather's eyes flew open at the sound of her mother's soft laughter. "Honey, don't feel like you're alone. Most girls chase after marriage like a dog chasing a car—and once they catch it, they don't know what to do with it. The idea of marriage is always different than the reality."

Heather sighed and rested her head on her hand, knowing truer words had never been spoken. In the past year, cold, clear reality had intruded into her rose-colored dreams so many times . . .

Christmas Eve was a prime example. She had worked so hard to make everything perfect. She and Kurt had decided that they'd spend Christmas morning with her folks and Christmas afternoon with his, but Christmas Eve was to be their special time. Though Heather had a pressing deadline for the newspaper, she told herself that she'd work double-time on December 26th to catch up.

So, on Christmas Eve morning, she rose early, tiptoed into the kitchen, and began to make Christmas dinner. She wrestled with the turkey—a twenty-six pounder, far too big for her and Kurt alone, but anything smaller just didn't look festive enough—and finally freed the drumsticks from the wire thingy that held the bird together. She mixed the stuffing, cleaned out the body cavity, then stuffed the breadcrumbs and onions and walnuts into the cavernous bird.

When the turkey was finally in the oven—and while Kurt was still sleeping—she began to make a pumpkin pie, Kurt's favorite holiday dessert. She couldn't find the pumpkin pie spice in the cupboard, so she doubled up on the cinnamon, figuring no one would know the difference.

By the time her sleepy husband came into the kitchen, she had the entire dinner in the oven and carols playing on the stereo. While he puttered around searching for coffee, she showered and dressed, choosing a very special outfit: jeans, a Christmasy velour sweater, and red and white socks with tiny jingle bells sewn into the cuffs.

While she put on her makeup, she rehearsed the afternoon. Their tree, purchased at the grocery store a week before, stood now in the living room, bare and unadorned. She would put a pot of apple cider on the stove, toss in a couple of cinnamon sticks, and pull out the Christmas cookies she had picked up at the bakery. While they nibbled on cookies and sipped cider, they would carefully unpack the ornaments Heather had brought from her home. She would tell Kurt the history of each wooden and plastic bauble from her childhood before lovingly placing it on the tree.

At her request, and as a special surprise for Kurt, his parents had sent a box of ornaments too, and Heather had resisted the temptation to peek inside. She wanted Kurt to tell her about each ornament, its history and heritage. Together they would build upon the traditions of their past and weave new and beautiful memories.

She put away her mascara tube as Kurt stumbled into the bathroom, his eyes more alert now than they had been twenty minutes before. Standing, she kissed his stubbled cheek and placed her hands on his chest. "Come into the living room after you shower and dress," she whispered, giving him a shy smile. "And we'll decorate the tree."

He grunted in assent, and Heather slipped away to begin her final preparations. Kurt never took long in the bathroom, so she'd have just enough time to put Amy Grant's Christmas album in the CD player and light the evergreen candle she had been saving for this very special occasion.

Ten minutes later, Amy was singing "Breath of Heaven," the candle was scenting the room with the heavenly fragrance of evergreen and pine, and cider steamed in two festive teacups on the coffee table. The two battered boxes of ornaments rested beneath the tree upon an embroidered tree skirt that had been her grandmother's. Heather sank to the carpeted floor in front of the tree and crossed her legs, grinning at the sound of the tiny bells on her socks. Kurt would think her socks were silly, but they'd still make him smile. And that's what this was all about, making Christmas special for him, her new family . . .

Ten minutes later, he still hadn't come out of the bedroom. Heather squirmed in impatience, then decided that he must be looking for his razor again. And since she had probably misplaced it, this wouldn't be a good time to call out and ask what was keeping him.

Ten minutes later, he still hadn't appeared. Heather drew a deep, exasperated breath, then told herself that he was looking for the special Christmas sweater she had bought him last year when they were only engaged. She had spent hours searching for the perfect red wool sweater, knowing he could wear it over and over again as they celebrated a lifetime of Christmases together.

To help pass the time, Heather lifted the lid on the dusty shoebox that held her old ornaments. She picked up a crocheted snowflake that her Aunt Irene had made when Heather graduated from high school. The white thread had yellowed a little, but the lace was still spidery and delicate. Next, she pulled out a small framed ornament, complete with baby photo and the words, "Heather's First Christmas." She smiled, wondering if Kurt had something similar. What fun this would be, if only he would hurry up.

She dropped her ornaments back into the box, then stood and walked to the bedroom, the tiny bells on her socks jangling all the way. She paused in the bedroom doorway, and what she saw took her breath away.

Kurt sat on the edge of the bed with his back to her. His hair was still wet, and he wore jeans, socks, and an old flannel shirt that had probably been around since the final episode of *M*A*S*H* aired on TV. He was leaning forward with his elbows propped on his knees, because his attention was riveted to the tiny television in the corner . . . and an ESPN report on the NFL playoffs.

Heather stood frozen in the doorway for a moment woven of eternity, then she spun on her heel and stalked back to the living room. Amy had begun to sing "Breath of Heaven" again, and the cider had stopped steaming long ago. The Christmas cookies would be moldy before Kurt willingly switched off ESPN.

Why had she bothered with any of it? Kurt obviously didn't care about Christmas traditions.

She crossed her arms, tears stinging her eyes as she stared at the bare Christmas tree. What should she do? She could march into the bedroom and demand that he come out, but belligerence would only destroy the mood she had worked so hard to create. And Kurt would be disgruntled if she forced him away from his sports. He would probably just toss the ornaments on the tree, gulp his cider, and hurry back to the ESPN report.

She could say nothing and decorate the tree herself, but what sort of precedent would that set? He would never appreciate a Christmas tradition he'd had no part of. Besides, Christmas was meant to be shared with the one you love.

As Amy Grant launched into the merry strains of "Jingle Bell Rock," Heather walked through the kitchen and took the stairs down to the basement. It took only a moment to find the circuit breaker panel, where Kurt had methodically labeled each and every switch. She found the one labeled "master bedroom" and snapped the black plastic lever to the left. Then she crossed her arms, leaned back against the washing machine, and waited.

Amy hadn't even finished her version of "Jingle Bells" before the basement door flew open. Kurt stood at the top of the stairs, his eyes wide with alarm. "Something happened to the TV," he said, staring down at her.

Heather turned to look directly at him. "I know."

"You know? How—what happened?"

"I flipped the circuit breaker."

"What?" Kurt double-timed it down the stairs, his eyes huge and disbelieving. "Why would you do that?"

Heather drew a deep breath and forbade her voice to tremble. "Because you were supposed to help me decorate the tree. I was waiting for you, I had everything ready, and you didn't come. You were too busy watching TV."

He squinched his face into a human question mark. "Why didn't you come in and tell me you were waiting? I'd have come out."

"I shouldn't *have* to tell you." Her voice was hoarse with frustration. "You knew I was waiting in the living room. You knew I wanted us to decorate the tree together. I had hot cider and cookies and a box of ornaments from your parents to surprise you. Good grief, I even had on jingle bell socks!"

Kurt smiled at her then, and in his eyes Heather saw surprise, confusion, and regret. "Honey, I'm sorry. I didn't know."

You should have known. She bit back the words she wanted to shout and let him pull her into an embrace, finally bending enough to uncross her arms and stiffly pat his back.

That touch seemed to reassure him. He released her and looked down into her eyes. "Can we decorate the tree now? And can we turn the power back on?"

She nodded stiffly, then led the way up to the living room while Kurt followed . . . but not before snapping the circuit breaker back into the on position.

The memory of that Christmas brought a wry, twisted smile to Heather's face.

"Is something funny?" her mother asked. "I think we could use some good news about now."

"I was just thinking about last Christmas," Heather said. "It was a good time, but in some ways I have never felt more alone. As I watched Kurt decorate our tree, I realized that as close as we were, we were still two different people, groping toward each other through a fog of misunderstanding. All that stuff about the two becoming one—well, it hasn't happened to us yet."

"Becoming one takes time, honey." Her mother reached out and patted her hand. "And nothing hurts us quite as severely as the hurts that strike at our hearts. But to love, you have to be vulnerable. You have to let the wall around your heart down."

Heather nodded, but at that moment she had never felt so intense a need to guard her heart.

Chapter Eight

Kurt's heart sank as he approached the house. There was no sign of Heather's Ford Escort.

He glanced at his watch as he pulled up and climbed out of the 4Runner. It was nearly two o'clock. Where was she?

He entered the kitchen and spotted the answering machine's flashing red light. He reached for it and hit the play button.

The mechanical voice responded, "You have one new message."

He waited for what seemed a lifetime as the machine rewound, beeped, then started to play: "Hey, Heather, Tiffany. Not much to say. Just checking up on you. Oh, did you hear ..."

With a heavy sigh, Kurt turned and opened the refrigerator as the message rattled on. Tiffany was one of Heather's many friends. And for not having much to say, the woman would no doubt go on forever. But where was Heather? What was she doing? What could possibly be—

Then another emotion hit. Not frustration, not resentment, but worry. Maybe something was wrong. Maybe she'd been so distraught over their argument that she hadn't paid attention to her driving and—

He slammed the fridge and crossed to the kitchen drawer where they stashed the phone book. After wasting valuable minutes searching for the Illinois State Police, Kurt called information, got the number, and dialed it. Another lifetime passed as he waited for someone to pick up. Finally, an all-too-cheery voice answered, and Kurt asked the dreaded question that had been taking over his thoughts.

"No, sir," the woman replied. "There have been no fatalities reported in your area."

"What about, like, serious injuries? Could there have been—"

"Nothing has been reported in the past several hours, sir."

Kurt's mind raced. "What about minor accidents? Do you have anything that could—"

"Sir, if your wife was in an accident, don't you think she would have contacted you by now?"

Kurt rubbed his temple. "Well, yes. Maybe. I mean . . ." He began to pace. "What if she hit her head really hard on the windshield—not hard enough for a major injury, but hard enough to get amnesia so she couldn't remember our phone number or who she was or—"

The cheery voice began to wilt. "Sir, believe me. If she was in an accident, you would have been contacted."

Kurt nodded. "Yes, yes, you're right. Yes, uh . . . and thanks. Thank you."

"And thank you for calling the Illinois State Police. Have a nice day."

Kurt hung up. He stood a long moment, not knowing whether he should be frightened, concerned, or just plain mad. Where was she? At a friend's? How about Jill's? No, Jill was visiting her parents for the week. Her dad had suffered some sort of heart attack and—wait a minute, of course! Her family. Heather always talked to her mom. Granted, the Irvins lived a good fifty minutes away, but still . . .

Kurt reached for the phone again, pressed the first button on the speed dial, and waited for the call to go through.

He'd always been mystified by how Heather and her mother could find so much to talk about. A day didn't go by that the two weren't in touch. If they weren't communicating by phone, they were talking by fax or e-mail . . . or sometimes all three the same day. He figured it was another one of those female things. As the oldest of three brothers with no sisters, female things were definitely not his area of expertise—a fact Heather's presence underscored every day of his life.

"I don't get it," he had asked one Saturday afternoon three or four months into their marriage. "If there's no problem, and it's not a special occasion, and there's no earthshaking news, what's the purpose of calling her?"

Heather laughed. "Calls don't need a purpose, silly."

Genuinely baffled, Kurt looked at her. "But if you don't have anything to talk about, what is there, you know, to talk about?"

"Life," she said, snuggling up to him on the sofa.

"Life?"

"You know, the little things. Like did Dad mow the lawn, are gas prices going up again, and when is Mary's daughter from next door going to have her baby? That kind of thing."

Kurt shook his head, still not getting it. "But I've seen you two go on for an hour."

She nodded. "Sometimes longer."

"Don't get me wrong," he said. "I think it's great that you and your mom are close, but . . ." He paused as Heather reached for the phone. "What are you doing?"

She began to dial. "Let me show you how it's done."

"Who are you calling?"

"Your mother."

"Heather, I just called her last week."

"I know, for her birthday. But you never call her just to say hi or to say you love her."

"I tell her I love her every time I call. I don't need to make a special—"

Heather motioned for him to quiet. "Hi, Mom," she spoke into the receiver. "It's Heather."

"Heather," Kurt whispered.

She ignored him. "Fine, just great. And you?"

He didn't know what she had in mind, but when he saw her mischievous smile he knew something was up.

"Good, we're good. Listen, Kurt and I were just sitting here talking about you, so we thought we'd give you a call."

Again he whispered. "Heather—"

"I know, it is sweet. But you raised a sweet son. Uh-huh." She laughed. "No, he never told me. Really? That is so thoughtful."

Kurt sighed wearily. Heaven only knew what secrets about his past were being revealed this time.

"Well, I'd better go," Heather finally said. "But Kurt's right here, so hang on a second." Before he could protest, she pressed the phone into his hand.

"What am I supposed to—"

"Just talk to her," Heather whispered as she pushed the receiver toward his face.

"But—uh, hi, Mom."

"Sweetheart!" his mother chirped, "How nice of you to call!"

"Yeah, well the weekend rates are a lot cheaper and—ow!" He rubbed the spot where Heather had just jabbed him in the ribs. "So how is everything?"

"Just fine, sweetheart."

"Good. That's good." Silently, he mouthed to Heather, "What am I supposed to do now?"

"Just talk to her!" she whispered.

"So, uh . . ." Kurt searched for topics. His mother was in good health, he and his brothers took care of any expenses Social Security didn't cover, and he'd even remembered her birthday. So what was left?

"Talk about life," Heather whispered. "Little things."

Kurt nodded, then suddenly motioned that he had something. Heather smiled and gave him a thumbs-up.

"So how are Toby and Ginger?" he asked, proud that he could remember the names of his mother's cats. "Still doing all those crazy, uh, cat things?"

Heather's smile turned to horror. She shook her head violently.

He made a face at her. What? He'd finally found something to talk about and now she was saying it wasn't good enough?

"Sweetheart," Mom answered, "Ginger's been dead nearly six months now."

Kurt blinked. "Really. Well, I'm sorry to hear that. You should have told us."

"I did. And you and Heather sent me that nice card, remember?"

"A card?"

Heather nodded broadly.

"Oh, right," he said, watching his wife. "We sent you a . . . sympathy card."

More nodding from Heather.

"That was so thoughtful."

"Yeah. Well, you know, that was mostly Heather's idea."

"I'm sure it was, dear."

He didn't remember much more of the conversation. There was something about the weather, and bunions, and a blouse sale at K-Mart. They finally ended with a detailed scene-by-scene account of the latest *Touched by an Angel* rerun. For all intents and purposes, that call had been completely pointless. A waste of time. And yet, on two separate occasions, his mother had mentioned how sweet he was to think of her and how much she had appreciated his taking the time to call. Amazing, how something so trivial could mean so much.

Now he leaned against the kitchen counter as her parents' phone rang in his ear. Yes, sir, the weird world of womanhood was a strange and fascinating place. And Kurt would have been totally oblivious to it if not for Heather. Already she was helping him become a better son. Already she was helping him understand things about herself, about himself, that he would never have begun to comprehend—

"Hello?" The sound of Heather's mother's voice jarred him from his thoughts.

"Hi, uh, Frankie, Mom."

"Kurt? Is that you?"

"Yes, ma'am."

"How are you, son?" Her voice seemed tighter than usual, as if she knew something was wrong.

"Uh, I'm pretty good. Listen, Heather hasn't called you or anything, has she?"

There was a fraction of a pause, then the answer. "She's sitting right here."

Kurt felt a wave of relief. He took a breath, then let it out. "She's okay then. I mean, she's not hurt or anything."

"No, she's just fine."

"Good, that's good. May I speak to her for a second?"

"Certainly."

At first he thought the rustling was the phone being passed from one hand to another, then he heard muffled voices and realized that a hand had covered the mouthpiece.

After several moments, he called, "Hello?" There was no response. He tried again. "Hello?"

"Kurt?" Heather's mother was back on the line. "Can you hold just another minute?"

"Well, sure, but—"

There were more muffled voices, this time a little louder and a little more passionate until Frankie came back again. "I'm sorry, Kurt. Right now is not a good time. Maybe you should try later."

"What?"

"Can you call back a little later?"

"I just need to talk with her for a second."

More muffled voices until she returned. "Um, Kurt—"

"Listen," he interrupted, "I know Heather and I are in the middle of a little disagreement, here, but—"

"Actually, son, I'm afraid it might be more than that."

The phrase brought him up short. "What do you mean?"

"Try a little bit later, okay?"

"But—"

"I'm sorry, Kurt. You know how fond I am of you."

What was she saying? "Look, if you could just put Heather on, I'm sure—"

"I'm sorry, son. I truly am."

Stunned, he stood at the counter with the phone pressed to his ear. What was going on? Surely things weren't that serious. Even if they were, they could be fixed. His training in management had taught him that if people were willing to communicate, anything could be fixed.

I'm afraid it might be more than that.

Was it possible? Had they really gone so far they couldn't communicate?

Suddenly a new thought arose, one he'd been trying to avoid all day. Actually, it whispered and taunted from the back of his mind whenever they had arguments. *Is this how it began with my parents . . . before their separation, before the divorce?*

"Kurt? Son, are you still there?"

"Yes, ma'am."

"I really think it's best if you call later."

All the wind had been taken out of his sails. With no course of action to follow and with no other argument to be made, Kurt swallowed hard. "I understand," was all he could say.

"Sometimes these things just take time," Heather's mother added. "But don't you worry, I'm sure you two will work everything out."

"Yes," he answered. He was on autopilot now. "I'm sure you're right." But for the first time in his marriage, Kurt Stone wasn't sure. And that frightened him. That frightened him very much.

After murmuring a toneless good-bye, he hung up.

I'm sorry, son. I'm afraid it might be more than that.

Slowly, he sank into one of the kitchen chairs. He was no longer certain he could stand.

Chapter Nine

Heather rubbed her hands against her jeans as her mother dropped the receiver back onto the phone. Unable to face the hurt in her mother's eyes, she pulled herself off the sofa. "I need some air," she mumbled, moving toward the front door.

What she really needed was time alone to think and weigh her options. Kurt had finally called, so he had come home, and he was trying to reach out. Now the decision was hers—should she call him back, make him wait, or accept the fact that they were lucky their marriage survived an entire year?

Standing in her parents' driveway, she thrust her hands in her pockets and looked up. The sky was pure blue from north to south, and the sun had just begun to dip toward the western horizon. There was still time to get home before dark. They might even still be able to keep their seven o'clock reservation at La Traviata, though she'd have to hurry if she wanted to do her hair and put on the little black dress she'd bought last weekend. The fitted dress was flirty and fun, just the thing for an anniversary, and just the type of dress Kurt liked her to wear.

But if she went home and dressed for dinner, she'd only be denying the deeper problem that had surfaced again this morning. She could accept Kurt's flustered apology, even knowing that he still didn't understand the forces that had driven her out of the house. She could go out to eat, smile, and pretend that everything was fine, but in a few months some other little thing would cause a big problem and the truth would smack her in the face again—they were just too different from one another to live in peace. If they couldn't celebrate an anniversary without their differences interfering, how were they supposed to raise children and grow old together?

If she didn't go home soon she might never wear that dress.

A metallic clanking sound shattered the hot stillness of the afternoon. Startled, Heather bent and peered around the hulking '56 Chevy that occupied the most prominent place in the driveway. The powder blue car had belonged to her father for years, and the amount of attention he lavished upon it would have made any woman but her mother jealous. Once, when Heather asked her mother why they didn't get rid of the thing, her mother smiled. "A man has to have something to do with his hands, Heather," she said, a glint of humor lighting her eyes. "A hobby. Some men golf, others fish, others chase women. I'm just glad your father's hobby keeps him happy and at home."

Running her hand over the flawless finish, Heather walked from the back bumper to the front. Her father was lying on the concrete beneath the car, grunting softly.

"You okay under there, Dad?" she asked, squatting down.

Her father let out another emphatic grunt, then inch-wormed his way out from beneath the car. "Fine, just fine." Without acknowledging Heather further, he raised the hood and bent over the engine.

Heather eased her back against the wall of the garage and slid down to the concrete floor. She could sit here all day without bothering her single-minded father; he was just like her in that regard. She could be at work on a project in her little office, and neither an explosion nor a house fire could break her concentration. Only Kurt could.

She frowned, reminded of yet another reason why marriage had brought more patience than peace. Kurt was always there. Well, not really. He did leave for work every morning at eight o'clock, and he didn't come home until after five. But when he was home he was always underfoot.

It didn't help that the guest room she used for an office had become their bedroom since they began remodeling the house. Now when Kurt came home, he stretched out on the bed and turned on the little TV, expecting her to go on working. Impossible! She could have handled the constant background noise, but the feeling of being watched strained her nerves. She couldn't even cough without Kurt asking, "You catching a cold?" And if she stopped clattering the computer keys to read something, he always assumed she had stopped working. So while she tried to think, Kurt felt free to tell her a story, ask a question, or make some comment about the television commercial . . . as if she had time to actually watch it.

She had tried to get her intensive work done early in the day so she could be free when Kurt came home, but she needed her daytime hours to at least try to pick up the house, run to the newspaper office, place and answer telephone calls, arrange appointments, attend staff meetings, eat lunch with her coworkers, and conduct interviews. By the time she had all her background work done, she almost always had only a few hours to write up her story. So she had to write at night, at home, and Kurt was anything but considerate of her efforts.

She certainly tried to support him in his work. She had attended the Kids 'n' Toys company Labor Day picnic and Christmas party, trying to have a good time while painfully making small talk with people she didn't know. While Kurt and a few of the other guys played volleyball at the Labor Day picnic, one of Kurt's coworkers made a pass at Heather. She brushed the guy off as politely as possible, and, in an effort to keep peace in Kurt's office, didn't even tell him about the incident.

She was doing all she could to help him succeed—but what was he doing for her? Some of her friends said she was lucky to have found a man who wanted her to succeed in her work, but wanting and helping were two different things.

Her thoughts filtered back to a night just last week. She'd been working hard on a profile on the new school board superintendent, and she had just two hours to polish and fax the piece to the news office. Kurt came in at five-thirty, tossed his jacket on the bed, and kissed the top of her head. "What's for dinner?" he asked, completely oblivious to her flying fingers.

Forced away from her thoughts, she gritted her teeth and stopped typing. "I haven't even thought about dinner."

She smoothed the irritation from her face as Kurt moved into her field of vision and sat on the edge of the bed. "Want me to pick up something? Or call for pizza?"

"What I want"—she held her fingers over the keyboard and cast him a lowered look—"is to finish this piece. I've got to have it in by seven-thirty. After that, I'll think about dinner."

Kurt didn't answer. He just stood, unknotted his tie, then tossed it on the bed next to his jacket. Without speaking, he left the room, and Heather assumed he would go watch TV in the living room.

She caught her train of thought and rode it for a full minute, typing furiously, then paused and looked at the bed. Kurt's coat and tie still lay there—mute testimony to the fact that something was wrong. It was unlike Kurt to abandon his clothes—if they weren't dirty, he usually returned his jacket and tie to the proper place in the closet within a minute or two. And no sounds came from the living room, so he wasn't watching television.

What was he doing?

"He's a grown man, he can amuse himself," she muttered, searching her notes for a quote from the school board super- intendent. "You need to get this article done."

She found the quote and typed it in, but her thoughts whirred and lagged, unwilling to move past Kurt. Groaning in annoyance, she got up and went in search of her husband.

She found him in the living room, lying in his worn recliner, his hands folded across his chest, his eyes closed. His face was expressionless—he might have been angry, hurt, or bored stiff.

"Kurt?"

His eyes flew open.

"Honey ..." She spread her hands and struggled for words. "I'm sorry if I was short with you. It's just that I'm under pressure, and I've got to get this article done. But I promise, at seven-thirty, I'll be all yours. Okay?"

He lifted one shoulder in a slight shrug. His expression didn't change, though Heather thought his eyes seemed slightly shiny and the corners of his mouth tighter than usual.

Heather ran her hand through her hair as she moved back to the bedroom. She had apologized, but Kurt didn't seem to think much of her effort. What did he expect of her? He knew she had to meet her deadlines. She had made promises to her editor, to the newspaper, and to the school board superintendent. She couldn't let those people down; this was her job.

"Ouch!" Her father's sharp cry brought her out of her musings. "Heather, I've cut my finger. Can you hand me one of those towels in my toolbox?"

"Sure, Dad." Heather reached over to her father's ancient toolbox and found a clean rag in the lower compartment. She held it out, then watched as he wrapped the soft fabric around the tip of his index finger.

"Is it bad?"

"Naw, nothing but a scratch. Just caught me by surprise, that's all."

Heather hugged her knees. Life had a way of catching you by surprise. If last week anyone had told her that she'd spend her anniversary at her parents' house contemplating the end of her marriage . . .

"You know, I'm glad I kept this car," her dad said, stepping back to admire the gleaming blue beast. "But there was a time—the years when she wasn't a classic, but just old—when I was tempted to sell her."

"Dad!" Heather's mouth dropped open. "I can't imagine you without this car."

"I coulda sold her." Dad held up his finger and grunted in satisfaction, then tossed the blood-smeared rag back into the toolbox. "The upkeep isn't easy, and replacement parts are awful hard to come by these days. But when my daddy gave her to me, he made me promise to take care of her. And so I have."

Heather made a face, remembering all the times she'd been embarrassed to be seen riding in her father's antique automobile. "Do you really think Gramps meant for you to keep the car? I mean, anyone would understand if you wanted to trade it in for something more modern."

Her father shook his head, then leaned forward to wipe a tiny smudge from the chrome bumper. "You don't understand,

Heather, money was tight in those days. My dad didn't have to give me a car at all; he was working hard just to keep food on the table. Buying a new car, and then giving it to me ..." His voice softened. "Well, that was a real sacrifice. I knew my father loved me, but I never knew how much ... until I saw what he was willing to give."

He cleared his throat, then leaned down and picked up a wrench. "Trouble is," he said, bending over the engine again, "big cars like this need constant attention. If I leave it for a day, it begins to rust. It guzzles gas like a hungry baby at the bottle, and goes through oil as fast as you can slap a tick. And you can't idle in this baby—when you're driving, you've got to keep one foot either on the gas or on the brake. It's a powerful thing."

Heather nodded, understanding why her father had never let her or Billy drive the Chevy.

"Some people might say I've wasted an awful lot of time tinkering with this car," her dad said, using the wrench to tighten something under the hood. "But I don't really care what people say. I made a promise to my father, and I'm going to keep it."

Heather propped her head on her hand. Her dad's consistent care of that car had been noticed by practically everyone in Peoria County—even the paper had noted it in a column on local legends. Her father was many things—opinionated, loud, and sometimes brash—but no one could deny that Henry James Irvin kept his promises.

"You see, Heather," her dad said, his voice coming at her from within the Chevy's dark mouth, "the only time this car hurts is when I get too busy doing other things to remember that she needs me. Every day, even if it's just a quick spot check of the engine or the paint, this car needs my attention."

Heather's mind, lulled to inertia by her father's deep voice and the warmth of the sun, exploded into sharp awareness. Why, he wasn't talking about cars at all! Her forthright father, who never had been able to face any emotional trauma head-on, was dispensing fatherly advice in the only way he knew how.

Her mother had always been the one to listen to Heather's problems while Dad puttered in the kitchen, eavesdropping in his not-so-sly way. Kurt would probably be the same kind of father, leaving Heather to handle the emotional upsets while he repaired broken bicycles and assembled science fair project boards.

Opposites. He and her mother were as opposite as salt and pepper, yet they had learned how to complement each other over the years. Maybe the process of two becoming one wasn't something that happened through the magic of love, but through the process of learning ... and bending. Of giving sometimes, and apologizing sometimes, and sometimes accepting that differences made life much more ... challenging.

She glanced up at her father, who had bent over the car again, as hesitant as ever to confront one of her problems. The car he had been speaking of wasn't a car at all, but her marriage, which required constant attention. He'd even been stressing the holy origin of matrimony, stressing that it had been given by a Father, out of love.

She smiled, sorting through her thoughts, then stood and moved to his side. "So, what you're saying"—she leaned on the car—"is that maintaining a car takes time and effort."

"That's right." Avoiding her eyes, he dropped his wrench to the concrete driveway, then bent to unscrew a grease-covered thingamajig.

"And if a person makes a promise," Heather went on, careful to use the right words, "he or she should work at keeping that promise every single day."

Her father stopped fiddling with the engine and straightened, then looked directly into her eyes. When he spoke again, his voice was gruff. "That's right, baby girl."

Heather rose on tiptoe, threw her arms around her father's neck, and gave him a squeeze. "Thanks, Daddy."

Chapter Ten

Waves of anger washed over Kurt, followed by sorrow, then fear, then anger again. The conflicting emotions churned in his chest until they formed a heavy knot. A year ago he would have only admitted to the anger. That's how he had always responded to pain. But now, thanks to Heather's influence, he'd become more sensitive to his feelings. Now, he could acknowledge the hurt. And he did hurt. A lot.

I'm afraid it might be more than a little disagreement.

How did it happen? How could things unravel so quickly? How, in just a few short months, could he and Heather have gone from committed lovers to people who wouldn't even communicate?

That's how it had been in his own family. He was only eight when his parents divorced. And, though he never admitted it, not even to Heather, he had always been terrified that the same thing would happen to him. *Terrified.*

And now . . .

I'm afraid it might be more than a little disagreement.

The words left him numb, almost sick, as he rose and ambled toward the plastic sheet separating the kitchen from the new addition.

Ah, the new addition . . .

He pushed aside the plastic and stepped into the unfinished room. This was to be their master bedroom. This was where they were to share their most intimate moments, to express the deepest possible communication between two humans. This was where they had planned to conceive their children and begin their family.

But now . . .

They'd been warned more times than they could count that additions and remodels were the greatest test for any couple. But they were mature adults, and more importantly they were deeply in love. If anybody could do it, they could. And what better way to draw closer to one another than to do it themselves? Heather had watched her own father build their house when she was a child, and Kurt had some carpentry experience between his sophomore and junior years in college. It certainly wouldn't be that difficult. Surely they could withstand a little inconvenience as they worked together to accomplish a little simple remodeling.

Unfortunately, he quickly found out that *little* was a relative concept. So was the word *simple*.

"It's just a square," she had said, as she stared down at his plans on the graph paper—his painstakingly exact, carefully drawn-to-scale plans.

"Well . . ." He cleared his throat, pushing aside any resentment that she didn't immediately gush over his work. "It's just a room, we're only enlarging a room."

"I know, but . . ." She let the phrase hang. He knew she was trying to be diplomatic, but it was obvious she wasn't pleased.

"But, what?" he asked.

"Nothing. I mean, it's fine."

"Fine? We're adding on 150 square feet to our bedroom, and all you have to say is it's *fine?*"

"I'm sorry, I just mean that it's not, well, you know . . . I mean, it's . . . fine. It's great, Kurt. It's great and fine."

"Heather . . ."

"I'm sorry, but it's just . . ." She searched for the right words not to hurt his feelings, but, of course, that had already happened.

"Go ahead," he said.

"Well, I mean it's a box. When you step back and look at it, it's just a box added onto a bigger box."

He fought back his impatience. "A box with a window seat, a bookshelf, and over here I've put in a drawer for our video cassettes, and see, here's the fireplace we talked about."

"You're right Kurt, it's nice, it's very, very nice."

"But . . ."

"It's a box."

"If you've got something else in mind, I'm open. I mean, this is supposed to be *our* project."

He could see relief suddenly fill her face. "Hang on just a minute." She disappeared, and a moment later she'd produced a sketchbook. "I've been doing a little doodling myself—you know, looking at magazines and getting ideas and stuff."

"Uh-huh . . ." Kurt nodded, pretending to be open, but already suspecting there was going to be trouble.

"I mean it's not to scale or anything," she said, flipping open the cover, "but it's kind of like a general idea."

At first Kurt was unsure what he was staring at. To be honest it looked more like a giant clover leaf than a room.

"You see, instead of straight walls, I was thinking we could have them curved, like this." She pointed to one of the leafs or petals or whatever they were. "And with three of these, even though we have one room, we actually wind up with three separate spaces." She motioned to the other two leafs. "Isn't this cool?"

"Yes, uh, cool," Kurt said, trying not to sound incredulous. "And what is this in the center?"

"That would be the fireplace."

"In the center."

"Exactly."

"And this?"

"The waterfall."

"The water—" He coughed, then covered it with a frown. "I thought this was indoors."

"Oh, it is . . . but only for a while. See, the stream goes under this wall over here and then out into the backyard and the lap pool."

"Lap pool."

"Of course we wouldn't do it all at once; we couldn't afford to. But it gives us something to work toward over the years." She snuggled in closer, admiring her handiwork. "So what do you think?"

And so it began . . . the frustration, the compromise, and of course, the added expense.

That had been five months ago. Now Kurt leaned against an exposed two-by-four and let out a heavy sigh. In many ways this room epitomized everything that was wrong with their marriage. He wanted practical and affordable boxes. She wanted harebrained, Taj Mahals.

Next came the construction phase. After going back and forth over the plans dozens upon dozens of times, they finally came to a compromise. Not sterile boxes, but not cascading waterfalls, either. It was more like a mini-atrium with a window seat. It had gone much slower than they had anticipated. In fact, after five months, they were less than halfway through, with just the foundation poured and the framing complete. But, even now, Kurt could see that it would be better than anything he could have dreamed up. Or Heather, for that matter. By combining their skills—her boundless imagination and his practicality—the two of them had come up with something far better than either could have accomplished on their own.

But it was more than just coming up with a great concept. The strength of their combined skills was also obvious in the execution.

Truth be told, Kurt wasn't quite the builder he thought he was. But he wasn't about to tell Heather that. Besides, this would be good for him—allow him to work with his hands, to be a man's man, just like Heather's dad. And if Heather had any doubt about Kurt's ability to measure up to her father, this would certainly put it to rest. So he read, he did his homework, and he bought all the right tools— $1,800 worth. "You can't do the right job without the right tools," he'd explained when he caught her gaping at the receipt.

Then came that fateful Saturday morning. They awoke at sunrise, Heather made coffee, and for the next two hours they chopped and dug and cleared the junipers away from the side of the house.

Finally, it was time to get down to the real work. Not, of course, without Heather's moral support. "Are you really sure this is such a good idea?" she asked as he emerged from the garage with his shiny new red sledgehammer. "I mean, shouldn't you double-check the plans or something and make sure there's nothing inside that wall?"

"Heather, guys do this all the time."

"I know, but—"

"But what?"

She lifted her hands and took a half-step back. "You're right. I don't want to spoil your fun."

"*Our* fun." Kurt grinned as he turned, testing the weight of the sledgehammer in his hands.

Heather nodded. "It's just that—"

He glanced back at her. "It's just what?"

"Well, shouldn't you at least check?"

He tried to hide his exasperation. "Heather."

"I know, I know. But you're an executive, not a construction worker. Maybe there's something in there that—"

"Sweetheart, men do this all the time. It's in our blood. You gals have babies and nurture them; we build things and blow them up." With that he hoisted the sledgehammer. "Watch and be amazed." He pulled the hammer back, swung hard, and with one swift blow smashed through the stucco. The resulting hole was quite impressive. If she had thought him some limp-wristed executive, well, he'd definitely shattered that stereotype.

But, instead of being awed by his prowess, she cried, "Kurt!"

"What?"

She shook her head, then tried unsuccessfully to nod in encouragement. She wasn't all that successful.

He covered his irritation by slamming a second, even bigger, hole into the wall. And then a third. If that overwhelming exhibition didn't silence her questions, nothing would.

Unfortunately, the third blow raised far more questions than it answered. That was the blow that struck the water pipe inside the wall, snapping it cleanly in two. The water pipe that began gushing like a geyser, spilling water inside the wall and out onto the bedroom floor. The water pipe that continued gushing until Kurt frantically searched for the main valve, finally found it, and tried to shut it off. His efforts would have been more successful if the valve hadn't been frozen, *and* if he'd had the right wrench, *and* if he hadn't used a wrong wrench to hit it several times, trying to loosen it, *and* if the valve hadn't broken off and crumbled into the dirt.

Other than that, everything would have been fine.

It was only after a $450 plumber's bill (the man insisted Saturdays were overtime) that Kurt finally conceded it might be better to listen to Heather's intuition a little more carefully.

But her involvement was far more than intuitive . . .

Heather had a unique gift for finding values. In fact, with her dogged determination in shopping, price comparison, and a certain amount of bartering, the inside of the addition was to be finished with materials Kurt had never dreamed possible—riverstone fireplace and hearth, an incredible mantel, wood floors, and the list went on. It truly would become their favorite place in the house—as cozy and creative as it was beautiful. And it would be theirs. The combination of *their* tastes, *their* talents, *their* personalities, *their* effort.

Suddenly, Kurt was struck by the realization. No! This room isn't what was *wrong* with their marriage. This is what was *right* with it. Hard? Yes. Frustrating? You bet. But like this addition, his life was also expanding. He was being made into something far greater, something far grander than he could ever become on his own. So was Heather. Together they were being transformed into something matchless, of exquisite beauty . . . something as matchless and beautiful as this room.

If they ever finished building it.

Kurt took in another breath and slowly let it out. Because if it was over, if they decided to call it quits and walk away, it would be like stopping the construction on this room—leaving it bare and unfinished. It would mean ignoring all of the room's possibilities, all of its potential beauty, choosing instead to leave it vacant and incomplete. Kurt swallowed back the tightness growing in his throat. Because it wasn't just this room that would be left vacant and incomplete.

It would be his life.

Chapter Eleven

"Mom?"

Heather jumped as the front door slammed behind her. She'd forgotten about that heavy oak door, it was so different from the quiet steel door at home.

Home. The word brought a lump to her throat. She glanced into the empty family room, then hurried toward her mother's bedroom. She had something to say before leaving.

She found her mother sitting on the edge of her bed, a framed picture in her hand. Heather knew without looking that it was one of her own wedding pictures, the candid shot her dad had snapped as she and Kurt sat in the back seat of the limo that carried them from the church to the reception. In the photo, she was holding onto her veil with one hand and Kurt's arm with the other. She and Kurt were both grinning like kids at Christmas.

"Heather." Her mother didn't look up. "It occurred to me that there is a way out of a troubled marriage. If things are really bad between you and Kurt, maybe you ought to consider it."

Heather stared at her mother in utter disbelief. "Mom, I'm not ready to—"

"Not divorce, not even separation." Her mother's voice was calm, her gaze steady as she looked up. "The way out is the way back to where you were a year ago. At your wedding, you put everything on the line; you gave Kurt your whole heart and life. In an act of the will, you threw caution and defensiveness to the wind, and placed everything you are and have in the hands of love. That's the way out of your trouble, Heather. You need to do that again."

Heather sank to her mother's side. "It's not that easy, Mom. We're carrying baggage we didn't have a year ago. We've hurt each other."

A faint light twinkled in the depths of her mother's brown eyes. "All couples hurt each other, Heather, especially in the early years when you're learning how to live together. But you can't look at those hurts as baggage—you should consider them blessings. They are lessons you've learned, and if you are wise, you won't have to learn them again." She smiled down at the picture and caressed Heather's image with her fingertip. "A year ago, you fell in love with Kurt. Now you might have to march into it. But love is your way out, Heather. It's the response God will honor."

"It hurts, Mom." The words slipped out before Heather could stop them. "I want to love Kurt, but I don't want to be hurt again. And I don't want to hurt him."

"'As iron sharpens iron, so one man sharpens another.'" Her mother's gaze drifted to the bureau, where another framed wedding picture stood, this one older and faded. "Sharpening is a painful process, Heather. But God can use it to make each of you into more useful vessels, useful to him and to each other. God loves you, but sometimes he chastens you, and sometimes you hurt him. But I haven't seen you trying to run away from God."

"I can't." Heather admitted the truth in a soft voice. "What's that psalm . . . wait, I remember. 'If I go up to the heavens, you are there; if I make my bed in the depths, you are there. If I rise on the wings of the dawn, if I settle on the far side of the sea, even there your hand will guide me, your right hand will hold me fast . . .'"

"Love is the same way." Her mother's brow wrinkled, and something moved in her dark eyes. "The love between a husband and wife should bind them as closely. It takes time, of course, but you have a lifetime to spend together. You could always give up and walk out, but the pain of that failure will never leave you. But the pain of sharpening fades into love, and will only draw you closer together. That's your way out, honey. Take your hurts, and determine to love each other better."

Heather sat silently for a long moment, her gaze resting upon the picture in her mother's hands. In the photograph she saw a giddily happy couple, the bride wedged beneath the groom's arm as if she truly belonged there.

The thought brought a twisted smile to her face. Hadn't God made woman from a rib taken out of the man's side? In the Garden, God closed up the wound, but marriage opened it again, positioning the woman at the man's side to fill the empty place in his life. Whether the man appreciated it or not, the woman wanted to be a lifelong resident of that God-designed space . . . which explained why she could no longer imagine living without Kurt.

Heather slipped her arm around her mother's shoulder and kissed her cheek. "Thanks, Mom, for being here when I needed you. I'm going to take off now."

Her mother looked up as Heather stood. "What if Kurt calls?"

"Tell him . . ." Heather paused by the door, then gave her mother a smile. "Tell him I'm coming home."

The traffic was heavy on the interstate, even for four o'clock on a Saturday afternoon. Heather slanted from the right lane to the left, dodging slower traffic while trying to keep her speed under the posted limit. The forty-five miles between her parents' house and Kurt's had never seemed so long.

At last she made her way out of a knot of traffic and settled back to coast in the right lane. Leaning back in the seat, she switched on the radio and felt her heart twist when the DJ began to play "The First Time Ever I Saw Your Face." Their song, hers and Kurt's. Could he be listening to it now?

Maybe. Since their wedding Heather had been surprised a number of times when they reacted to some situation in the same way at the same time. They were a long way from being able to finish each other's sentences like some long-married couples, but she couldn't deny that a bond existed between them. They were so much more than friends.

Her mind drifted back to January, when Kurt and two coworkers had to take a three-day business trip to Chicago. She had tried to act like it was no big deal; after all, executives traveled all the time. But she had nearly burst into tears when Kurt left the house, and that first night she did cry when she climbed into their bed, alone for the first time since the wedding. She used Kurt's pillow that night, breathing in his scent as she counted every tick of the alarm clock and tried to sleep.

Kurt and the others left for Chicago on Monday morning. They were supposed to spend Monday afternoon and all day Tuesday in meetings, then drive home Wednesday morning. After her wretched and mostly sleepless Monday night, Heather went to bed early Tuesday night and was lulled to sleep by the low-pitched voices of ESPN's sports reporters.

Abruptly, she awoke from a sound sleep and sat up in bed. The glowing green numerals on the clock read 12:45, and the sports guys at the ESPN anchor desk were mumbling something about an athlete in trouble for drug abuse.

Heather glanced around the dimly lit room, her nerves tensing as she searched for whatever had jarred her from sleep. In the television's soft gray glow she couldn't see anything unusual, but something had awakened her.

For no reason she could name, the dim white outline of Kurt's tennis shoes in the closet raised the hairs on the back of her neck. *Pray for him,* an inner voice urged, and without further hesitation Heather clasped her hands together and lifted her gaze to the ceiling. "Heavenly Father, I don't know what's happening, but be with Kurt. Wherever he is, whatever he's doing, keep him safe." She closed her eyes and repeated the prayer, murmuring the words over and over in an effort to dispel the gnawing certainty that something was definitely, undeniably wrong.

A moment later, the tension in her heart eased. Heather exhaled in relief, murmured a prayer of thanks, then reached over and pulled Kurt's pillow close. She closed her eyes as she lay back and hugged it to her chest, wondering if she would remember any of this in the morning.

The jangling of the bedside phone brought her fully awake again. She reached out and picked it up.

"Heather?" From the echoing sound on the line, she knew Kurt was calling from his cellular phone. "Honey, it's me. I just wanted you to know we're okay."

She took a deep, quivering breath to calm her pounding heart. "What happened?"

Kurt's voice held a note of awe. "We worked late, and I talked the guys into driving home tonight instead of waiting until tomorrow. We were fine, making good time, then all of a sudden a car on the other side of the Interstate crossed over the median and came right toward us. I didn't have time to brake, and somehow I swerved, and the car missed us by inches." He hesitated a moment, and when he spoke again, his voice trembled with stunned disbelief. "Honey, if that guy had hit us, we'd have been totally wiped out. I was going seventy, and there's no way we could have survived that kind of crash. Charlie and Tom are still shaking."

Heather closed her eyes as a feeling of warmth flowed from her head to her toes. *Thank you, God, thank you so very much.* She gripped the phone more tightly and smiled through a veil of tears. She wanted to tell Kurt about her prayer, about knowing that he'd been in danger, but the story could wait . . . until he was back in her arms, safe at home.

"I love you," she whispered. "Come on home."

"I'll be there before you know it, hon," he answered. "I just had to tell you—and I wanted to hear your voice."

Heather went back to sleep that night knowing that God had bound her and Kurt together with cords of love. The next morning they marveled over the story, and they shared it with only a few trusted friends. Some things were too private, too sacred, to share with the world.

Yes, marriage had turned out to be far more than she expected. It had been disruptive, occasionally intrusive, and had often thrust her into swirling unknown waters. But she had discovered treasures in the unknown, and there were further mysteries to explore . . . if Kurt could forgive her for walking out.

Heather flipped on her turn signal and steered the car toward the exit that would lead her home.

Chapter Twelve

❦

"Love is patient, love is kind. It does not envy, it does not boast, it is not proud. It is not rude, it is not self-seeking, it is not easily angered, it keeps no record of wrongs."

Sitting numbly on the sofa, Kurt watched Pastor Harrison perform their wedding ceremony. The fact that he actually managed to find the videotape of their wedding amid the hundreds of other tapes Heather had collected was a miracle ranking right up there with parting the Red Sea. Dear Heather loved to record television shows—bits and pieces from *20/20* or *60 Minutes* or whatever news event happened to be breaking at the moment. "I'm doing this for our kids," she would say as she pulled out another tape. "Our children will need these historical moments for their school reports and projects."

At first Kurt protested, explaining that any real significant events would surely wind up in the library or on the Internet. But he soon realized he was fighting an impossible battle.

His bride was an incurable pack rat, a fact conclusively proven when on the third Saturday after their marriage he tried, unsuccessfully, to drive past a garage sale. Over the months he really had strove to indulge Heather's penchant for recording every news event, holiday special, and Brady Bunch reunion, but he finally drew the line when it came to recording *Barney* reruns.

Pastor Harrison continued, *"Love does not delight in evil but rejoices with the truth. It always protects, always trusts, always hopes, always perseveres. Love never fails."*

Kurt had heard the Scripture dozens of times throughout his life, and both he and Heather thought it would be great for the ceremony. But now, for the first time, he really heard the words. And now, for the first time, they carried a stinging rebuke. If this was the real definition of love, then for years he'd been clueless about the subject.

Wasn't love supposed to be those warm heart-flutters, that inability to keep her out of his mind, that wonderful feeling of fullness he'd get just being in her presence? That was certainly what he'd seen on TV and in the movies. And that's what he had experienced himself . . . at least in the beginning. But this definition of love was something entirely different.

Pastor Harrison began reading from another passage. *"Wives, submit to your husbands as to the Lord. For the husband is the head of the wife as Christ is the head of the church, his body, of which he is the Savior. Now as the church submits to Christ, so also wives should submit to their husbands in everything."*

Kurt's guilt turned to anger. Of course, that was it. That was the problem right there—Heather's refusal to submit. How many times had she ignored his suggestions and insisted on doing things her way? And what did the Bible say? What did the pastor just read? *"Wives should submit to their husbands in everything."*

Everything. Not in some things. Not in most things. But in *everything*.

No wonder they were having such problems. No wonder their marriage wasn't working. The answer was right there in the Bible, in plain black and white. Heather was not obeying. She was not *submitting* to him.

Unfortunately, Pastor Harrison's reading from that passage wasn't quite finished. *"Husbands, love your wives, just as Christ loved the church and gave himself up for her to make her holy, cleansing her by the washing with water through the word, and to present her to himself as a radiant church, without stain or wrinkle or any other blemish, but holy and blameless."*

Kurt's anger disappeared as quickly as it had surfaced. There was that word again—*love*. But it was a love he still did not understand. It wasn't a love that gave because of the good feelings it brought. It wasn't a love that spoiled his wife so he could receive warm fuzzies in return. No, this was a different type of love, a love that *gave himself up for her* with no strings attached. A love that *gave*, warm feelings or no warm feelings.

Kurt took a hesitant breath. God had instructed him to love Heather, yes, but to love her *as Christ loved his church.*

A caring love, a nurturing love, a doing-what's-best-for-her love. And, if necessary, a dying love. That was the type of love that led Christ to the cross. Obviously Jesus felt no tender, feel-good emotions as they crucified him. He experienced no warm fuzzies as they drove the nails through his feet and hands, no heart flutters as he looked down upon their mocking and taunting faces, and no feelings of contented joy as he died a horrific death. And yet it was . . . love.

Kurt's throat grew tight as his eyes filled with moisture. Their problems weren't Heather's fault, they were his. *He* had failed. Since the beginning of their relationship *he* had loved her with a love that was best for *him*. Even when he gave, even when he sacrificed, it was still for *him*.

"Do you, Kurtis Anthony Stone, take Heather Michelle Irvin to be your lawfully wedded wife?"

At the sound of his name, Kurt looked back up to the TV. On the screen was a younger Kurt, a more naïve Kurt—a self-centered, self-confident young man who thought he could do anything, including be a husband.

The pastor continued his question. *"Do you believe God has brought you together and led you to give your lives to each other in love?"*

The younger Kurt turned to Heather and looked earnestly into her eyes. So ignorant he was. So selfish.

"Will you give yourself to helping Heather reach her full potential as a person created in God's image?"

As he continued watching the ceremony, Kurt's throat ached with emotion. The tears spilled onto his cheeks.

"Will you cherish her with tender love just as Christ loves and cherishes his bride, the church?"

Kurt did not hear the groom's answer. Instead, he was surprised by a heaving sob that escaped somewhere deep within his gut. Another followed, almost as strong. Before he knew it, he was crying. He tried to stop, but he couldn't. How could he have been so arrogant? So full of pride? Give himself up for her? There was no way he could love like that. Who did he think he was?

No longer able to stand the pride, the hypocrisy, the lies, he fumbled for the remote control and shut off the TV. Now there was only silence. Empty. Condemning. Heart-crushing silence.

"Kurt?"

At first he wasn't sure he'd heard her voice.

"Honey?"

He turned and there was Heather standing in the doorway. He had no idea how long she'd been there.

"Heather . . ." His voice was thick with emotion as he rose to his feet. He wanted to race to her, to throw his arms around her, to apologize for every selfish act. But he didn't move. He wasn't sure he could.

"Would you turn it back on?" she asked hoarsely. "The TV?"

He stared a moment, then nodded and reached down and fumbled with the remote until the picture filled the screen. Once again Pastor Harrison was speaking. *"Heather Michelle Irvin, do you take Kurtis Anthony Stone to be your lawfully wedded husband?"*

Kurt stared at the image of the beautiful bride, so innocent, so trusting, as she looked into her bridegroom's eyes.

"Do you believe God has brought you together and has led you to give your lives to each other in love?"

He heard Heather move from the doorway and approach the sofa. He was careful not to look at her.

"Will you give yourself to helping Kurt reach his full potential as a person created in God's image? Will you be faithful to him and care for him as the church is loyal to Jesus Christ?"

The young bride answered, *"I will."*

But, standing there beside him, near the sofa, Heather quietly whispered, "I can't."

He finally turned to her. Tears were streaming down her cheeks as well.

"I'm sorry," she repeated. "I can't." She took a trembling breath. "I don't . . . I don't know how."

He wanted desperately to reach out to her, to comfort her, but he fought back the temptation. At that moment he was as lost as she. Instead, all he did was nod and softly croak, "I know . . . neither do I."

She moved a tentative step closer, and he could no longer resist. Before he could stop himself, his arm reached out and wrapped about her. Instinctively, she moved in, filling that special Heather-shaped space under his arm. The two stood together like that, lost in their memories, watching the idealistic couple say their vows, listening to them make impossible promises that neither could keep.

When the couple on the screen moved to light the unity candle, Kurt finally cleared the thickness from his throat. It was time to ask the question—the one he dreaded, but the one he knew he had to ask. "So . . ." He coughed again. "Where do we go from here?"

Heather turned slightly, but she still did not look up at him. "I guess," she said, the fringe of her lashes hiding her eyes, "we take the only way out."

The knot returned to Kurt's chest. He tried to swallow but couldn't. When he thought he could trust his voice, he asked, "Are you sure?"

She nodded. "Mom and I talked about it. She said the only way out of a troubled marriage is to go back to the moment we surrendered our lives to each other." Heather reached for Kurt's free hand and held it in her own. "It's like when we became Christians, how we surrendered our lives to Christ. Marriage is pretty much the same thing, a process of loving and surrendering—to each other, and to God."

Relief washed through Kurt. He took a deep breath and felt the heaviness start to lift. Fear and that suffocating tightness in his chest began to loosen. He raised his wife's hand. He turned it over, looking at it, seeing how small and fragile it looked inside his own.

Surrender.

Was it really that simple?

A process of loving and surrendering.

He continued to gaze at her hand. Surely, there had to be more than just *surrender*.

And yet . . . isn't that exactly what he tried to do with the other areas of his life, surrender them, turn them over to God? Years of experience had taught him that there was no way he could endure the pressures at work, the day-to-day disappointments, the thousand and one migraine-makers of life—at least not on his own. And if he couldn't succeed in day-to-day living on his own, what made him think he could possibly succeed in marriage? What made him think he could possibly be a husband without turning that over to God as well?

"So . . ." She finally looked up at him. "What are we going to do? Quit . . . or surrender?"

Kurt looked into her brown eyes. Those deep, dark pools that had captured his heart. Eyes so vulnerable yet so full of compassion.

"We surrender," he finally whispered. Then swallowing, he continued, "To God . . . and to each other."

A smile of relief flickered across her face and he was immediately pulling her into his arms. They were both crying again. Soon each was telling the other how sorry they were, confessing how selfish they'd been, how self-centered they were. Kurt wasn't sure how long they held each other like that before Heather finally pulled away—just enough to lift her mouth up to his. And then they kissed. Softly. Tenderly. He could taste the salty tears on her lips, tears mixed with his own. When they separated, they looked deeply into each other's eyes.

So much love there. So much caring.

Movement on the TV caught his attention. "Look," he said. She turned and there, on the screen, the couple was also kissing. And when they parted, Pastor Harrison spoke for the final time. *"Ladies and gentlemen, it is my great privilege and joy to present to you Mr. and Mrs. Kurtis Stone."* The recessional began, and the two newlyweds started down the aisle, radiant and beaming.

Kurt glanced at his watch. "Listen," he said. "If you want we can still make it to La Traviata. Our reservations aren't until—"

Heather pressed her finger to his lips, and he came to a stop. "I've got a better idea," she said. "Why don't we just stay in tonight. Maybe order a pizza, just the two of us."

Kurt smiled. "Yeah, we could do that." But, unable to resist, he added, "Or we could pick it up in the Toyota and maybe do a little off-roading on the way back to the—ooff!"

Her elbow landed squarely in his gut and stopped him cold.

"Hey," he protested, "it was just an idea." Then, growing more serious, he added, "Actually, I was thinking we could go back to the dealer tomorrow and see if we can get something a little closer to your tastes."

"Like a minivan?"

Kurt couldn't help cringing. "If that's what you want. But you don't exactly strike me as the soccer mom type."

"Appearances can be deceiving. Then again, appearances can reveal everything . . . if you look carefully enough."

Kurt frowned. "What's that supposed to mean?"

"I didn't finish giving you all of your presents this morning."

"You didn't?"

She shook her head. "Come back to the addition. I want to show you what you didn't see earlier."

Heather took his hand and Kurt allowed her to lead him out of the living room, into the kitchen, and through the plastic sheet, into the unfinished room. It was just as bare as it had been earlier, but it was no longer empty. In fact, with Heather there, it was filled with life.

She walked to the center of the empty space. "You know this reading area we've been talking about?"

Kurt nodded.

"I think we can utilize the space more efficiently."

"Efficiently?" He stared at her in surprise. "Isn't that my word?"

She threw him a smile. "Wait here. I'll be right back."

Kurt crossed his arms, watching in bewilderment as Heather pushed the plastic aside and disappeared through the doorway. In a moment she was back, carrying the photo collage she had given him earlier that morning.

She held the frame for him to see. "We began here," she said, pointing to a photo of them on their first date. "And over here we married." She pointed to a wedding picture. "And here we honeymooned . . . if you call the Alaskan wilderness a honeymoon."

"Hey . . ."

She shrugged good-naturedly. "It's all pretty clear. Here are the photos of the house, you and your sledgehammer, me holding my first published article as Heather Irvin Stone."

He followed the pictures, nodding while trying to follow her thoughts. Heather's creativity frequently caught him off guard, and often he wasn't sure where she was going.

"And here—" She moved closer as she pointed to the last photo, the one of her with the silly red bow tied around her waist. "That picture is my last present to you." There was a short silence as her words hung, obviously waiting for a response.

Kurt looked to the picture, then to her, then back to the picture. Finally, he shook his head. "I'm sorry, honey. Call me dense, but I don't get it."

She squeezed his arm. "Think, Kurt."

He thought, then took a plunge. "You're giving me you? I mean, all over again?"

She smiled. "You've always had me."

He looked back to the picture, studying its layout, searching for some clue. Finally he sighed. "I'm sorry, Heather. I'm just not . . ."

"All right, let me give you another clue. I'm not thinking about a sitting room anymore, but something else. Something painted all in blues . . . or maybe in pinks."

Kurt chuckled. "What type of person would paint a room all in blues or pinks? Those colors are more for—"

The answer crashed into his mind like a freight train. He blinked, then took a deep breath as a dozen different emotions ran through his head. "Heather—that's not something to joke about."

"Who's joking?"

"You—you mean—you're—we're—" Odd, that a college graduate couldn't articulate a single sentence. "Baby?" he finally gasped. "We're having a baby?"

"Very good. I knew you'd catch on." She casually strolled over to the beginning of the new addition. "And the doorway to the nursery would be just about perfect here."

"Heather!" In a half-dozen steps Kurt was behind her, embracing her. Soon, he lowered his hand to her stomach, still flat, but shielding a new life.

She lifted her head and turned to meet his eyes. "Are you happy about it?" she whispered.

"Happy?" He turned her, then held her. "Yes! Of course I'm happy!"

But, even now, as he held his wife, his thoughts began to churn and whirl. A thousand concerns, a thousand new worries flooded his mind. If marriage had expanded him before, who knew what becoming a father would do? Could he handle it? What about the responsibility? A helpless human being entirely dependent upon them? For everything? Was he really ready for that?

Yet, even as his fears rose, a certain peace began to settle. For Kurt already knew that the answer to his concerns was identical to the answer to his marriage.

Surrender.

He could not do it on his own. He would need help. Like

everything else in his life it called for a love greater than his own. But, regardless of the inevitable trials and heartaches and mistakes, he knew he could make it.

They could make it.

Love asked for everything . . . and, with God's help, Kurt was ready to surrender everything. Yes, he would continue learning how to love his wife. Yes, it would be a lifelong process. But now, with the help of heaven, he would also learn how to love his child.

That's what Kurt Stone hoped. And, as he held his wife in his arms, that's what he began to pray.

Also by Bill Myers

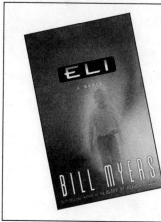

Eli
Softcover 0-310-21803-9
Audio Pages 0-310-23622-3

Don't miss Bill Myers's Fire of Heaven Trilogy

Blood of Heaven
Softcover 0-310-20119-5
Audio Pages 0-310-21053-4

Threshold
Softcover 0-310-20210-9
Audio Pages 0-310-21571-4

Fire of Heaven
Softcover 0-310-21738-5
Audio Pages 0-310-23002-0

Pick up a copy today at your favorite bookstore!

ZondervanPublishingHouse
Grand Rapids, Michigan 49530
http://www.zondervan.com

A Division of HarperCollins*Publishers*

We want to hear from you. Please send your comments about
this book to us in care of the address below. Thank you.

ZondervanPublishingHouse
Grand Rapids, Michigan 49530
http://www.zondervan.com